AFTER THE CRASH

AFTER THE CRASH

New Investment Strategies for Survivors from America's Foremost Financial Experts

DONNA SAMMONS CARPENTER

CB
CONTEMPORARY BOOKS
CHICAGO · NEW YORK

Published by Contemporary Books, Inc.
180 North Michigan Avenue, Chicago, Illinois 60601
Manufactured in the United States of America
International Standard Book Number: 0-8092-4525-6

Published simultaneously in Canada by Beaverbooks, Ltd.
195 Allstate Parkway, Valleywood Business Park
Markham, Ontario L3R 4T8 Canada

CONTENTS

Acknowledgments

This book could have been written without the help of Abby Solomon, but it's hard to imagine how. Thanks are also due to Helen Rees and David Sammons and to all the folks at Contemporary Books—Bernie Shir-Cliff, Kathy Willhoite, Mary Mack Eley, and Donavan Vicha.

AFTER THE CRASH

Introduction

It felt like the end of the world—and, in a sense, it was. The crash of the U.S. stock market on Monday, October 19, 1987, heralded the end of business as usual.

For investors, large and small, the historic 508-point drop in the Dow Jones Industrial Average marked the end of one era and the beginning of another.

"It was a little like seeing an atom bomb go off," Richard R. West, the Dean of New York University's Graduate School of Business, told reporters. "Once you've seen it, you know it could happen again. The world has changed. It will never be the same."

Dallas billionaire H. Ross Perot agreed. It was "God tapping us on the shoulder," he said, "a warning to get our act together before we get the big shock."

The collapse of the market, and its wild gyrations since, are now a national obsession. The only constant is uncertainty. No one, it seems, knows what to do next.

That's where *After the Crash* comes in. *After the Crash* provides you with the information you need to invest your money wisely in the wake of the market collapse.

The book does not rely on one person's limited knowledge. Rather, it draws on the intelligence and experience of the nation's top financial experts.

The book presents—in roundtable format—the insights of these experts from the country's leading financial institutions and academic centers.

They show you how to adjust your strategies as the economic climate shifts, and they lay out ways for you to shield your portfolio from future danger. They also show you how to profit—regardless of whether the market goes up or heads down.

Shall we begin?

Part I

ASSESSING THE DAMAGE

1

GAZING IN THE CRYSTAL BALL

Where Have We Been? Where Are We Going?

What caused the crash of 1987? Who saw it coming, and what did they see? Does one crash mean there will be another one soon?

Are markets more uncertain now than they were before Black Monday? Is the economy? And, if so, what should investors be looking for?

So many questions.

If the crash accomplished nothing else useful, it reminded us that uncertainty is every investor's unbidden companion. We need to remember that even during the long run of a strong bull market, we ignore uncertainty at our peril. Smart investors—and those who advise them—keep on asking questions.

We've probed the thinking of more than a dozen of the country's most alert minds—academic and institutional economists, top executives, and money managers—to find out what they knew before the crash, what they saw coming, and what they see ahead now.

If you think the crash of 1987 was a fluke, you're wrong. Powerful forces still at work will keep the volatility of financial markets high.

To thrive—even to survive—in the market in the near-term, investors will have to hone their own questioning skills. They better know what to ask, whom to ask, and how to act on the answers.

There's no better place to start, we'd suggest, than with the questions we put to these preeminent economists, financial-service executives, and market analysts.

Excerpts from an interview with Peter Anderson, senior vice president of IDS Financial Services, a subsidiary of American Express, based in Minneapolis, Minnesota.

"What we saw on Black Monday was this: We saw in ten days a stock market decline that normally takes two years. So, in my mind, the decline is really behind us, not in front of us. To be selling stocks at this point is a reaction to October 19 that I think is folly.

"I'm bullish on financial instruments—be they fixed-income instruments or common stocks. Let me explain briefly why I am bullish.

"Number one, I think that we're going to have an ideal economic environment over the intermediate term—that is, for the next 18 months.

"I don't believe we're going to have a recession. I don't believe we're going to have a boom. Rather, I think we're going to have a long period of very modest growth, in the area of 1 to 2 percent, and very little inflation—on the order of perhaps 3 to 4 percent.

"In that environment, we're going to have the Federal Reserve consistently follow a policy of monetary ease. If you follow this kind of policy in an environment where economic growth is sluggish, you get a decline in interest rates.

"Finally, the big surprise is, corporate profits are going to be extraordinarily strong for the next few years, despite the fact that we're going to have sluggish growth.

"Normally, in an economic environment of 1-percent growth, you get about a 10-percent decline in earnings reported on the S&P 500. This time, I think if we have 1-percent growth, we'll have a 10- to 15-percent improvement in profits. That's never occurred before.

"Why do I hold that view? When you get an economic slowdown, earnings declines don't come across the board. They come in cyclical industries.

"In other words, earnings don't decline at McDonald's and they don't decline at Dun & Bradstreet. They decline at US Steel, Alcoa, and Dow Chemical—cyclical industries.

"This time, we've got a different kettle of fish. The complete and utter collapse of the dollar has made these highly cyclical companies extraordinarily competitive.

"And I think that you're going to see such a tremendous surge of exports that we're not going to see the usual volume declines that we see in these industries. Also, prices will hold up, because capacity utilization will be higher.

"So both prices and volume will do extraordinarily well. And instead of earnings declining in these industries, they should surge in the next two years.

"Where do I see the Dow heading? Over the next two years, we will not only return to the 2700 plus level. In my book, in two years we'll be over 3000.

"Now, I don't want to leave the impression that I think this market is going straight back to 2700 in the next month or two. We are not. You can't do what you did to people on Black Monday and expect the market to head right back up.

"I think we're going to have a series of rallies followed by a decline, followed by a rally, followed by a decline, followed by a rally.

"But each rally will terminate a little bit higher than the previous rally. And each bottom will terminate a little bit higher than the previous bottom.

"The market will be accompanied by fairly high levels of volatility. But, if you draw a line through this sawtooth pattern, that line is going to be clearly up."

Excerpts from an interview with Carolyn Shaw Bell, the Katharine Coman professor of economics at Wellesley College in Wellesley, Massachusetts.

"Nobody knows precisely what caused the market collapse, but concerns abroad about United States indebtedness had a lot to do with it. That's not the only factor, of course, but it's the one I'd like to focus on.

"The United States is now the largest debtor in the world and how this country will be able to meet payments on its debt is a matter of some concern. If foreigners think that these debts will not be repaid, they will want to pull their money out of this country. To some extent, that has already begun, and it contributed to the crash.

"Foreigners have invested in the United States in two ways. They have bought financial securities—not only United States government securities but corporate stocks and bonds, short-term money-market instruments, and just plain bank deposits.

"The second way foreigners have invested here is even more significant. They've bought out companies in this country.

"Many publishers, for instance, are now owned by foreign owners. The Sony Corporation of Japan has agreed to buy the record division of CBS. The Japanese and the Swiss have put money into real estate. Canadians own a large part of the American paper industry.

"And this type of foreign investment, which the statisticians call direct investment, has been increasing substantially over the past five years. In 1985, there was four times as much private, foreign capital invested in this country as in 1980.

"Both the ownership of real assets, such as factories and firms, and financial assets, such bonds or stocks, will require the future payment from this country of dividends and interest to the foreign owners of these assets. These payments will be a new and continuing drain on our economy, one that we have not experienced before. The closest analogy I can think of is the 1972 oil-price shock.

"So, part of these foreigners' concerns is that we won't be able to make these interest and dividend payments to them. That contributed to the crash.

"So did foreign concerns about the inability of Congress and the President to devise a deficit-reduction plan. The only way we have been able to afford such large budget deficits for the past five years without a substantial rise in interest rates is that foreigners have sent us a lot of their savings.

"We have not financed government spending by our own savings. We have let other people do the saving for us, and that is going to catch up with us.

"Here's what I mean. By 1990, our total foreign debt probably will amount to $700 or $800 billion. The interest and dividends on a sum like that will come to something like $56 or $60 billion.

"Now, last year we spent $60 billion to import foreign automobiles. We spent a little bit more than that to import oil. Okay, so we spent the money, but we got the oil and the automobiles in return.

"By 1990, though, we're going to be spending the same amount of money and getting nothing for it, because it will just be debt payment.

"The foreign contribution to the market crash may have been caused as much by their anticipation of future problems as by response to current U.S. economic conditions.

"Assume, for instance, that a German owns stock in IBM. The Germans are worried about the United States' economy, and they are afraid of two things.

"They fear that the budget deficit issue will not be settled and that U.S. interest rates will go up. If they do, the United States economy will slide into a depression, and IBM won't make profits. So the German investor says to himself, 'I think I'll sell IBM now.'

"The other thing foreigners fear is the falling value of the dollar on the foreign-exchange market. The German thinks to himself that other foreigners will want to pull their short-term capital, their bank deposits, out of the United States because they fear the shrinking value of the dollar.

" 'If they do,' he thinks, 'my IBM stock is going to be worth less, so I should sell it now before the value of the dollar falls any further.'

"Once you have people anticipating a fall in the value of the dollar, there is inevitably pressure to sell, which reinforces the expectation that the dollar will fall.

"If the administration can engineer a gradual decrease in the value of the dollar instead of a freefall, then there is some hope for avoiding disaster.

"A gradual decline would, in fact, be good. If we are going to make any headway on reducing the international debt, Americans must change their habits of buying abroad.

"If the dollar declines, for instance, I may be more interested in buying a Ford instead of a Toyota, because the Toyota will be more expensive than it was when the value of the dollar was higher.

"If, however, the dollar were to fall 20 percent in a single day as the stock market did—and it could, you know—we would have a disaster. Some financial institutions would fail, and a lot of people would be hurt.

"That's the kind of disaster scenario that nobody likes to think about. Nobody will predict that it's going to happen, and neither will I.

"But I will point out that if you had suggested 15 years ago that there could be an international financial collapse, any responsible economist would have said, 'Nonsense, that couldn't happen.' Now there is a finite probability that it could.

"I don't mean, now, today, as a specific consequence of the market crash. I'm not predicting a financial disaster. I just mean that, in general, now and for the past couple of years, it has been possible to think about such a thing, whereas 15 years ago you would have been wasting your time.

"A sudden plunge of the dollar could bring another crash not only on the stock market, but on money markets as well. Remember that when the stock market crashed October 19, the bond markets were not affected much. A dollar collapse, however, would affect both markets.

"The combined crash would affect a lot of small banks, insurance companies, and all kinds of institutions where ordinary people keep their savings. The government presumably would step in somehow, but I don't know exactly how.

"The Fed is, of course, the lender of last resort to the banks. Maybe the Fed and the FDIC could prevent people's savings in banks from being lost, but there is no way that anyone could prevent a huge loss of asset value in the event of a complete collapse.

"Putting that possibility aside, however, I still believe that people in the United States are going to be worse off in the foreseeable future in the sense that we will have fewer goods and services to use for our own benefit.

"We'll be able to consume less than we have been enjoying in the past five years, because we have been living that good life at somebody else's expense. There is no question that people will be travelling abroad less, buying fewer imported blouses and shoes, making do with American products whether they are equal in quality or style to the foreign goods.

"There is no question that taxes will go up in some form. I don't care whether they want to call them payments-in-kind or some other fancy word, taxes will go up. Just paying interest on the government debt already is the second largest expenditure in the federal budget after national defense.

"As for the international debt, eventually the United States is going to have to run a surplus on its balance of trade in order to service this debt while keeping it from growing. That means not just reducing the balance-of-trade deficit. It means turning it completely around. We'll need a $60-billion surplus just to pay our interest—more if we're going to reduce the debt principal.

"Either imports have to be reduced by that amount or exports have to increase by that amount or some combination of both. That's a very, very big adjustment, and everybody's going to be worse off. There's no avoiding it.

"If we have a gradual decline in the value of the dollar and a gradual adjustment to the fact that we've got to make these payments overseas, then maybe it will mean simply that people won't get the bonuses and the salary increases they got last year. Maybe it will mean that just a few more people are out of work.

"But the other scenario, the international collapse, could just as readily happen. And if it does, then millions of people will be out of work.

"Even if the dollar does decline gradually and we avoid the international collapse, there is no way we're going to grow our way out of this. That's what has been so dreadful about Reagan and his people all these years. They have been telling outright lies about how the United States economy will grow and the budget deficit will be reduced that way. You can't do it.

"Say that we had a balanced federal budget. We would still face the drain of making $60 billion worth of payments overseas every year without getting anything like automobiles or blouses or oil in return. That kind of drain on income is going to have a contracting impact on the economy as a whole.

"The price of imported goods will go up. People accustomed to buying imports will notice it immediately. But you won't have to buy imported goods to be affected.

"The price of imported raw materials and component parts will also go up, which means that the price of goods manufactured in this country from foreign materials will go up. Soon, the consumer price index will go up.

"People can react to this eventuality in one of two ways. They can demand higher wages to pay for this higher cost of living. That will give us an inflationary spiral, and it's the least useful way of bringing about the adjustment that has to take place.

"The other way is that people can start spending less and saving more. It means settling for a somewhat smaller house than you hoped for, giving your high-school senior a trip to the Southwest instead of Europe for a graduation present, making all sorts of small adjustments in the way you live.

"But at least this way you don't have the additional problem of seeing inflation wipe out the value of your savings or your pensions, which is awfully scary.

"In any event, in the near term, certainly in 1988, I don't see any reason to predict prosperity. Either we'll begin an inflationary spiral or a slight recession—or both. There are so many scenarios that we economists could invent for you, but I think these three are the most likely.

"For the longer term, I think the presidential election is going to be extremely important. Unfortunately, none of the presidential candidates is going to dare predict what I have just been telling you is going to happen. No politician is going to be able to say that, and if we elect a president who doesn't understand these things, then, well, you can draw your own conclusions.

"It's almost impossible to exaggerate the importance of our trade balance problem. It's the first time in history, except for Great Britain after World War II, that a rich industrialized country has been in debt to the rest of the world.

"During World War II Great Britain spent its assets, literally. People who owned stocks in foreign countries, people who owned bonds of foreign governments were asked to turn these over to the British government. And they did. They sold their capital to pay for fighting the war.

"We are selling our capital to pay for what? A bunch of wasted government deficits? It's a shocking thing.

"I don't see any reason why this country must go into a decline forever. It all turns on whether we can elect a competent president and Congress and whether we can get the kind of international cooperation that is needed. We can't fix everything alone.

"The Japanese, for instance, are currently preserving their high rates of employment by keeping export levels high. They could reduce their exports and still keep employment up by expanding their domestic economy, reducing the saving rate there, letting people have more goods and services, and building more housing. To a lesser extent, the same is true of Germany, the other large surplus country.

"If they both expanded their domestic economies, then the adjustment problems not only for this country but the rest of the world would be considerably ameliorated.

"The probability, however, is that if the United States begins exporting more because the dollar has gone down in price, other countries will try to protect their own markets. And, if that happens, then the global economy will shrink and world production will decline. The position of the Third World countries will become worse and—I don't even like to talk about it.

"If you want to forget about doomsday and predict heaven, imagine what could happen if spending on defense in the Soviet Union and in this country were cut in half. You would immediately release people and materials for other uses, and the prosperity of the whole world would increase. You would immediately be able to make resources available to the Third World countries.

"If we could get over our rabid fear of communism under everyone's bed, we'd be better off. I sometimes wish people would remember that we had a revolution in this country all by ourselves before Karl Marx was born. It's still possible to have revolutions without Communism."

Excerpts from an interview with Stanley H. Breitbard, national director, executive financial services, Price Waterhouse, a Big Eight accounting firm based in New York City.

"Here's the major lesson of the crash for me. It should drive people back to an inward focus. It should teach us that the important thing is focusing not on the market but on our own personal finances, on establishing a rational, long-term plan for dealing with those finances.

"Another lesson we learned from the crash is how truly volatile the market can be.

"You have people who for the past five years only made money in the market. They've always seen the good side of the market. But the crash demonstrates that there's just as great a probability that the market will retreat on the downside. And just as the movement on the upside is extreme, the retreats will be extreme.

"All the charts certainly demonstrate the market's tremendous volatility. That's why we can't say it too many times. In measuring return, you have to balance risk.

"The crash has reemphasized for us some of the fundamental truths of financial planning. Putting your financial affairs in order and maintaining that order requires tremendous discipline and patience, a sense of calm, and a sense of perspective.

"Most people find it difficult to avoid picking up the financial section of their newspaper each day to see how their investments are doing. There's something about human nature that makes us want to do that. But from a financial planning perspective, you have to take a longer-term view.

"People have to understand that on paper they may have lost 23 percent in the crash, but if they were invested in the equity market from 1981 through 1986, they probably averaged a compound annual rate of return of 12 to 15 percent per year.

"And when you look at the equity markets and at the risk and return ratios, it's more reasonable to assume that you're going to earn 12 to 15 percent over a long period of time than assume you can continue to get the 30 percent or 40 percent per year that people enjoyed in the last couple of years."

Excerpts from an interview with Jeremy G. Duffield, a senior vice president of The Vanguard Group of Investment Companies in Valley Forge, Pennsylvania.

"As you've no doubt been told by others, the market crashed because of substantial deterioration in the economic fundamentals, at least as perceived by the marketplace, and because of rising interest rates and the lack of progress on the trade deficit. These seem to be the most compelling reasons.

"Of course, the budget problems have been lurking for a long time. Yet, people finally seem to have caught up to that—and to the fact that interest rates had risen substantially, threateningly—in the preceding several months.

"The stock market had been on this roller coaster ride upward since the beginning of last year, paying little attention to basic economic factors.

"In retrospect, I think the market was probably overvalued. I think the events that actually set off Black Monday, however, were most notably, portfolio insurance and program trading.

"It wasn't a surprise that there was a correction, but the speed of that correction certainly surprised me.

"I wouldn't compare Black Monday to 1929. The economy is fundamentally sound. We can muddle through problems such as the trade deficit. I think that 1973 and 1974, when there was a real correction in the overvaluation in the marketplace, is a pretty good analogy for this market.

"As I said, the economy remains quite strong. The weaker dollar is favorable for U.S. exports. Interest rates have fallen to a level at which they should not act as a dampener to economic activity. Consumer confidence doesn't seem to have been affected dramatically by the change in market valuations. Investors are still not that far behind for the year just passed. I think the prospects for the economy are quite reasonable.

"The only danger I see that might push us into a recession is the Federal Reserve taking its foot off the peddle.

"At some point they may have to support the dollar again.

That may cause some tightening of the money supply, which could cause interest rates to rise, and that would be the thing to worry about.

"The other thing you might worry about long-term is whether we'll get more inflation from the growing money supply and from the weak dollar, which will cause import prices to rise.

"Deflation, contrary to what you might hear, is not going to be a problem at all. Consumer prices are still rising. Commodity prices have picked up. I think consumer prices will continue to rise. I'd say that we're in a period of low inflation, and the danger is that we could go into a period of moderate inflation.

"If I were an investor, I would pay attention to what the Fed is doing and consequently to what is happening to interest rates. To the extent that people can monitor these things, it's a useful exercise.

"There's a positive note to the crash in the sense that it removed some of the excesses. I don't think it's fundamentally sound to have an economy that is driven by speculative fever. It's not good for the economy. It's better when people have more realistic expectations."

Excerpts from an interview with Steven G. Einhorn, partner and co-chairman of the investment policy committee at Goldman, Sachs & Co. in New York City.

"It is almost impossible to offer today a forecast that looks out a year or more. All we can do is evaluate circumstances as they currently exist. And, as they exist, I am not inclined to advise our clients to put money back into the market. That may change, but as I look now, I see no reason to put money back.

"Why? First, the economy will have to slow down, we think, in 1988 as a reflection of the decline in stock prices. A lot of consumer net worth was extinguished in this market crumble, and we think that fact will be reflected in less consumer spending, and therefore a much slower economy.

"Second, we think earnings expectations are too high for 1988 and that analysts will have to revise their expectations downward.

"Third, the market, though it is not as grossly overvalued as it was back in the summer of 1987, is still not compellingly undervalued.

"Typically, these bear market declines, before they end and allow for the start of a new bull market, require that shares get to a compelling level of undervaluation compared to interest rates and earnings, dividends, and book value. We are not there.

"Those are some of the reasons we have not felt it appropriate to recommit our cash reserves. So we are sitting with those reserves, and, when circumstances allow us, we'll get back in. But those circumstances are not yet present.

"Bonds—intermediate-term bonds—seem attractive to us. We think interest rates can come down, and we think there are capital gains to be earned in the bond market over the course of the next six months to perhaps as long as nine months.

"We still have some equity exposure, clearly, and that exposure, though small, is in the defensive and interest-rate-sensitive sectors of the market—tobacco, foods, electric utilities, insurance, regional banks, drugs, and health care.

"And we have some interest, although not significant, in some of the export-related cyclicals that would benefit from a lower dollar—some stocks in the machinery area, such as Caterpillar and Ingersoll-Rand.

"One lesson of the market collapse is that value ultimately will assert itself. The market was terribly extended relative to all historic benchmarks.

"It had to be corrected, even though many, at the time, never thought it would be. So one lesson is, don't ignore value—or ignore it at your own peril.

"A second, and perhaps more important, lesson is that the market has a finite tolerance for inadvisable monetary and fiscal policies. The reason why the market ultimately did come down was because it viewed monetary and fiscal policies here and abroad as inadvisable.

"The policies that needed to be put in place to correct our trade deficit were expansive money policies abroad and tighter fiscal policies here. What in fact the market was getting was tight money abroad and expansive fiscal policy here.

"The third lesson is that international cooperation between

ourselves and our major trading partners is critical. We now live in a world that is interconnected.

"We depend on the savings flow from abroad to fund our budget deficit here. They depend on us to buy their exports and grow their economies.

"I think it was a bit surprising to some, but, when our market crumbled, every market around the world crumbled by near or like amounts. We are now linked much more tightly than any of us realized."

Excerpts from an interview with Robert Eisner, the William R. Kenan Professor of Economics at Northwestern University in Evanston, Illinois.

"There are two lessons to learn from the crash. One, that kind of thing can happen to markets. Two, we should avoid foolish fights either to keep up the value of the dollar or to fight non-existent inflation by the wrong means through raising interest rates and a tight monetary policy.

"I blame the fall of the stock market on rising interest rates and the evidence that the Federal Reserve, increasingly under Greenspan, was going to keep interest rates high—if not rising—in an attempt, apparently, to keep the value of the dollar from falling. That tactic was foolish and contributed to the crash.

"There are always warning signs that you see afterwards. The market had several bad days before Black Monday, and the rising interest rates were very troublesome.

"People just needed some trigger to make them feel that it must be going down and, therefore, they better get out or try to get out.

"Of course, not everyone can get out. They have to sell the stock to somebody else. Everybody tried to sell and nobody wanted to buy.

"I wouldn't be looking for another drop like Black Monday's. But if the Federal Reserve again raises interest rates and seems to be more worried about pleasing bankers and keeping the dollar up and fighting an inflation that doesn't have anything to do with excess spending, that can trigger a further drop.

"Of course, there are always dangers on the international scene. Some suggest the Japanese market might fall on its own, and that would trigger other falls.

"But I have no reason to think it will fall more. I have no reason to believe that stocks are generally overvalued.

"I might add that the budget deficits we keep hearing about, in my view, have nothing to do with the crash. Nobody ever really explains that point except to say that, in principle, anything that's bad must be bad for the market. Well, if anything bad must be bad for the market, then you may as well blame AIDs or crime.

"When the deficit has increased, the Dow Jones has tended to go up. If you relate the change in the Dow Jones and the change in the deficit, you find that changes in the deficit are associated with increases in the Dow.

"If you trace through and try to figure out why, there are various conjectures. But essentially, when you increase the deficit, if it's not due to a recession itself, you tend to stimulate the economy. Increasing the deficit tends to increase demand, increase production, increase profits. Whether people look at the deficit or not, they see the results, and when they see the results, the market goes up.

"The solution for the economy at this point? Easier money. Deficits are for the long run too large, and the mix is wrong. There should be a somewhat tighter fiscal policy and an easier monetary policy. And that's for the long run. The long-run target might be to keep the debt from growing any faster than the gross national product. People may differ with me about what to do about the deficit.

"The deficit did not contribute to the crash. Our theories indicate that markets react to new information to a large extent. The only new information that had come out about that time was that the deficit was way down by about a third.

"So, if anything, you could reason that the fall in the deficit was contributing to keeping the economy sluggish and a sluggish economy contributed to the crash. That theory certainly would be consistent with the data that I found for the past that say falls in the deficit were associated with falls in the Dow."

Excerpts from an interview with Benjamin M. Friedman, a professor of economics at Harvard University in Cambridge, Massachusetts.

"Sooner or later, the market was bound to take the dollar down to a level that would allow the United States to compete again. And, for the most part, that decline is good.

"But there are some drawbacks in the short run, one of which, of course, is the risk of inflation. The second one is that a disorderly dollar decline could create all sorts of threats to the stability of the financial system.

"I would be surprised if we had out-and-out deflation, because at this stage of the business cycle, there is already some built-in inflation. Until October 19, most people thought it was somewhere between 4 and 5 percent.

"Moreover, most people expected that rate to drift upwards, and the debate was about how rapidly it would build up. Now, in the wake of October 19, the outlook is clouded for a variety of reasons.

"Most people expect the economy to be weaker in 1988, which would decrease inflationary pressures. But a continuing decline of the dollar will increase inflationary pressures.

"It's difficult to judge which of the two will predominate. But I expect that, for the next year or so, the net effect of all this will be that inflation will be less than it otherwise would have been. However, that is a far cry from saying that prices will be falling.

"Some people believe that the same kinds of changing attitudes that led investors to reduce what they thought stocks were worth on October 19 also will lead the public to reduce what they think other assets are worth. If that happens, the implications for an economic downturn would be much more severe.

"Take, for example, house prices. There are many more homeowners than people who own stocks. Consequently, a decline in housing prices, for example, would directly affect many more people than a decline in stock prices.

"It's simply too early to say whether the price movement in stocks was a phenomenon unique to stocks or whether it's the opening round of a reduction of asset prices generally.

"As you know, the period of the last five years, when we've

had such rapidly rising stock prices, has also been a period of major appreciation in house prices in most of the major residential areas around the country. So lots of people have houses that are worth more than they paid five years ago.

"If house prices start coming down, that would have very serious ramifications for the economy. Many people would find themselves unable to borrow against their home equity, for example. People expecting to sell houses would find no market at a price that they consider acceptable. They wouldn't move, and they wouldn't build new houses.

"Another serious problem would be a cutback in consumer spending. We know that, historically, stock market declines are followed by lower consumer spending.

"What we don't know is whether it's going to be a large cutback or a small cutback. Part of the reason we don't know is that we don't know whether consumer spending had yet adjusted to the fact that stock prices were way up. After all, even after the Dow had fallen, stock prices were still higher than a year ago.

"The dollar has now come down very far, very fast, and our export performance is improving. At the same time, our imports were already rising quite dramatically. The net effect of these offsetting trends is still unclear.

"And there are other unanswerable questions. What direction will mortgage rates take? What is the business community going to do with its rate of investment?"

Excerpts from an interview with A. George Gols, chief economist for Arthur D. Little in Cambridge, Massachusetts.

"If there is a lesson to be learned from the stock market collapse, it is this one: We cannot live forever on credit. Eventually, the bill comes due.

"Never in the history of this country—except during Colonial times—have we been in a position where we had such a massive debt situation with our trading partners and found ourselves in such a tough competitive situation in the world. Also, the average consumer has never had so much debt.

"I'm forecasting a recession.

"And I think this recession will differ from any recession that's come before, because we've foreclosed the use of traditional measures to stimulate the economy.

"We cannot, for example, use deficit spending. In the past, we pumped up government spending when the private market started to slacken. That's precisely what we can't do because we've spent the hell out of ourselves in the good days. We've used up our reserves to do so this time around.

"The only relief that is available to us is to let the dollar drop lower, so we can boost our exports. But that would endanger the whole international monetary system."

Excerpts from an interview with Monte Gordon, director of research for Dreyfus Corporation in New York City and a regular on Public Television's "Wall Street Week."

"At the moment, deflation is more of a threat than inflation. Deflation would mean a lowering of our standard of living, a slowing of corporate profit growth, and a slowing of economic growth. It would put something of a lid on the ability of the market to recover strongly, because of the uncertainty that deflation would introduce.

"On the other hand, markets climb during recessions in anticipation of the recession's end. So, in the latter part of 1988, the market could be quite strong.

"I believe what you should do now is prepare for the recovery, take advantage of the decline. You've got stock prices coming down. You've got better valuation standards. Multiples are lower. Companies are showing reasonable earnings.

"Stock prices are way off from where they were, and if you take a long view, historically, this period will prove to be an attractive buying opportunity.

"But you must take a long view.

"I think investors have become more realistic. They had a giddy kind of a ride, and they enjoyed it, and they recognized that it wasn't going to last."

Excerpts from an interview with Maury Harris, chief economist for PaineWebber, an investment bank in New York City.

"We thought the GNP was going to grow 2.5 percent in 1987

on an annual calendar average basis. Now, we've cut that estimate down to 1.8 percent.

"The only reason we've revised our forecast is the effect of the market crash on the economy. A 1.8 percent growth in GNP is below average, but it's not a recession.

"One effect of Black Monday has been to teach individual investors about their vulnerability. Yes, there were forecasters who said that the market was overdone, but nobody ever thought it was going to go down so fast that people couldn't get out.

"The stock investor comes away from that experience, not so much scared away from the market, but feeling less secure. Since it happened once, it could happen again. It's something like being only slightly injured in a very bad automobile accident.

"People saw what they'd made in the market during the year just disappear overnight. So, in the future, they're going to feel a lot less secure about that kind of money, knowing that it may not be there when they need it. They can't count on it.

"People thought they were protected. The little guy puts his stop orders in, right? You know what happens on a day like Black Monday? You blow right through the stops.

"Brokers used to say, 'Don't worry. The most you can lose is 10 percent. I've got a 10-percent stop under it.' If you bought a stock at $40, and you have a stop at $39, the stop says you get that price or the next transaction's price.

"But when you're blowing through those prices, there may not be a trade between $40 and $37. People found out that the stops don't always protect them.

"You come out of this not saying that you'll never invest in stocks again, but knowing that an investment in stocks isn't like a nest egg that you can count on. Things can happen so quickly that you don't have time to get out. That's going to make investors a lot more cautious about how they feel about this kind of money.

"One good thing may happen, partly as a consequence of Black Monday. I think the savings rate will go up. High-income families who were counting on the stock market now know that they can't count on it like they used to."

Excerpts from an interview with C. Bruce Johnstone, managing director of Boston-based Fidelity Investments and portfolio manager of Fidelity's Equity Income Fund. He also serves as senior vice president and income-growth group leader for Fidelity Management and Research, a subsidiary of Fidelity Investments, in Boston.

"I was startled by the severity of the crash, not the direction. It had to startle anybody.

"What's my market outlook for the next 12 months?

"We don't have a market outlook *per se*. If I had a market outlook that was worth the paper it was written on, I wouldn't need a job. If you spend all your time trying to assess where the market is going, you might improve your odds for accuracy from 50/50 to 53/47. That's about as good as anybody gets. So why waste your time?

"It *is* clear to me that consumer spending is likely to be less robust than it would have been prior to the crash. Investor confidence and consumer confidence have been shaken. That's inevitable.

"And, therefore, big-ticket items are going to move more slowly than was the case before October—specifically houses, expensive cars, and expensive consumer electronics equipment.

"Slower consumer spending will undoubtedly have an effect on economic activity in general. Whether or not it's sufficient to drive us into recession, I don't know.

"To assess what may happen with the economy, people should look at automobile sales, housing starts, and housing permits, which really is an early indicator. Also they should look at retail department store sales, a figure that gets reported once a month. And I'd also look at the weekly requests for unemployment insurance and the once-a-month help-wanted indicator.

"The stock market itself is probably the most important economic indicator. If the market holds or goes higher, that's very bullish for economic activity. If the market goes down through the October 19 lows, that's very bearish.

"It's ironic. Usually the market is just a symptom. It takes the temperature of the economy. But now, I think, we're tenuous enough in terms of investor and consumer confidence that the market in and of itself can determine economic activity.

"The market is attached to the economy like a rubber band. And if the market goes up or down, the rubber band will stretch and pull the economy up or down with it.

"The first few signs of economic slowing might give the market a little jiggle on the downside. But since the market has already discounted some slowing—maybe even a mild recession—you'd have to see some fairly significant bad economic data—for example, a 20- to 25-percent drop in auto sales—to drive the market lower from an economic point of view.

"But there are other factors that can drag the market down.

"Japan is one. There's a real-estate and a stock-market bubble in Japan, and if it pops for whatever reason it can bring our market down as well. A third and related factor: If confidence in the dollar were not restored at all, if the dollar collapsed, we'd be in trouble.

"You don't necessarily have to bring the dollar up. But you don't want it to crash, because it would have such negative consequences. If you crash the dollar without giving foreign economies, such as Japan's and Germany's time to adjust, you crash their economies. And if you crash their economies, you crash their markets. If you crash their markets, we're in the soup."

"I'd judge a crash by the speed of the decline. It's not an absolute number. We could devalue the dollar 5 to 10 percent per year for several years and not bother anybody. But if we lost 20 to 25 percent of the value of the dollar in a month or two, that would be a disaster."

Excerpts from an interview with Douglas M. Loudon, managing director for Scudder, Stevens & Clark, which is based in New York City.

"This crash was different from ones we've experienced in the past, because it heavily involved the futures and options markets. Futures and options didn't cause the decline, but the combination of them and program trading accelerated it.

"Typically, this kind of decline would take six to nine months. So, if we got it all over in a month and a half, that's great—and a lot less painful.

"We at Scudder disagree with those who say the crash is going to lead us into a recession. We're not wildly optimistic, but we don't think we'll have a recession.

"We think we were on the verge of an economic boom when the crash occurred. In fact, the third quarter GNP numbers were very strong and would support that contention.

"So the crash knocked us off what would have been an acceleration of growth. Now, we're back into the kind of sluggish, irregular growth that we'd been having anyway.

"Of course, this is the first time that we've really had a global equity market. And the decline just worked its way all the way around the world. All the markets went down. They went down by different amounts, but they all went down somewhat.

"What concerns us most, in that context, is the impact the crash may have on global growth. It illustrates again, as some people have been saying for a time, the necessity for global integration, for governments and monetary authorities in different countries to work together.

"The United States is in a higher risk situation, because we are now net debtors. We're now more exposed financially. International coordination is really a necessity to make the whole thing work and get back on a sounder footing.

"But we do think this has been a Wall Street panic rather than a Main Street panic. We've seen some indications of that contention in terms of spending patterns after the crash. This crash was unusual, because the public wasn't hurt nearly as bad this time around as has been the case in the past.

"If you look back over the last five years, in spite of an acceleration in the sale of equity-mutual funds this year, probably five times as much money has gone into fixed-income funds. So the ratio in equities didn't get high enough to hurt the average individual.

"On the institutional side, most pension funds were overfunded going into the decline, so it's not going to hurt them much. The ones who did get hurt are, as far as we can see, the index or risk arbitrageurs. That doesn't bother us. We don't feel sorry for them.

"So we think the crash will probably knock three-quarters of a percentage point off the GNP over the next year. But if it were true to historic norms, it would be more like 1.5 percent. Then you're getting close to the point where you can talk about recession. But we just don't think that's going to happen.

"People thought it was a new era. You get a market that goes to a new all-time high and the valuation parameters say the market's high, and people say, 'No, it's different this time and here's why its different.'

"And this time around, it was primarily the thought that the dollar had declined to an extent that we were going to have a real surge in manufacturing profits—which will come sooner or later. That's still ahead of us. That's a positive.

"The concern we have is that if global growth slows down, even with a weaker dollar, U.S. manufacturing companies will probably have a bigger slice of a slower growing pie.

"So it almost washes out. It's still a net positive, but not nearly as positive as it would have been under the projections being made a few months ago."

Excerpts from an interview with John D. Markese, vice president and research director for the American Association of Individual Investors in Chicago.

"The crash happened for a variety of reasons. Primarily, it was a sell-off caused by a long market rise and a lot of basic fundamental values being pushed to their limits—values such as price/earnings ratios, price-to-book-value ratios, and dividend yields.

"Americans started looking at five to six years of a run-up and at all the fundamentals being pushed to, or beyond, historic limits for value. I also think institutional selling and the derivative, or futures, markets helped start the fall.

"Once it broke through, programmed trading and portfolio insurance just got a wave of selling going, and it didn't stop. Everyone was basically trying to protect the profits they had to that point, and a lot of soothsayers were saying that the end of the bull market was clearly about to happen. So when there was a break everyone said, 'Well, it's finally here.'

"That's all it was in my opinion. It wasn't economics. It was not an economic crash. It was a market crash. But it throws into question where we're going from here. It clearly means that the market has a great deal more volatility than anyone had believed in the past.

"Now, everyone knows that there could be another 500-point day. And if we do have a dramatic down day, it could move to a massive down day again. We live with that fear. We've now educated everyone to the fact that a 500-point day is possible.

"Also, the market seems to take information on the economy anyway it wants to. In other words, the weak dollar is good, the weak dollar is bad; raising taxes is good, raising taxes is bad. So I don't think any of the actions we take are going to do anything we can predict with certainty.

"If, however, the market for some reason goes through previous lows—if it ever went through 1738 again—I think we'd have massive selling. We could go all the way down to 1400 or 1500 or so.

"That's simply because a lot of people are looking at charts. I don't believe in charts. But if everyone acts on them, there's a real possibility of another drop. And more people are looking at charts than have ever looked at them before, because whenever you have market volatility, people turn to very mechanical tools.

"The market is, in many ways, a function of investor expectations. It could have gone from 2700 to 3300, then dropped back to 2700, and everyone would have said that was a crash.

"I give a lot of seminars and most individual investors I speak to are looking long-term. Anyone who wanted to sell has sold. People are now going to hunker down. I don't think they're going to get out until we see what we believe to be the end of the financial world as we know it.

"But the institutional trading is back. Everything is back. And not a whole lot has changed. So we have the potential for a lot of volatility yet."

Excerpts from an interview with Richard J. Piket, a vice president of BankAmerica, which has its headquarters in San Francisco.

"I don't think the public understands the ramifications of our debt problems. Shakespeare said, 'Neither a borrower nor a lender be.' You start there.

"You create debt and you create risk. Once somebody borrows money, and they don't have the money in hand to pay it back, there's an element of risk. The whole world—this country in particular—has gone on a debt binge. And it has to be resolved.

"The numbers don't lie. You look at trade deficit numbers and budget deficit numbers, and you look at the business borrowing and you look at the consumer borrowing and the lack of savings, and you know there's a high degree of risk in the financial system.

"We have to reduce that risk."

Excerpts from an interview with Francis H. Schott, senior vice president and chief economist for The Equitable in New York City.

"All year, the market appeared to be overvalued. It was going outside the range of normal price-to-earnings ratios, dividend yield, and book-to-value ratios.

"You could find similar P/E ratios twenty years ago, but it hadn't happened since then. And I couldn't think of a really good reason it should happen now.

"But I also thought that, with the Japanese pouring so much money into our market, it actually could continue to work. That is still a possibility, by the way.

"In discovering our market and seeing that our market is much lower value than the Tokyo market, the Japanese might pour so much money in that it could eventually lead to some more or less permanent higher valuation of our stocks.

"I would have more nearly believed that the Tokyo market would have gone down while ours went up. That didn't happen. It turned out that the two markets were linked on the up- and downsides. And the overvaluation of Japan relative to other stock markets persists.

"By my calculations, the market has now returned to a normal range, particularly with respect to P/E ratios. They should be around 16.

"Are we likely to see another 500 point drop in the Dow? The question reminds me of people who ask me for doomsday scenarios. One has to specify the assumptions that lead to doomsday. It doesn't happen in a vacuum, just as October 19 didn't happen in a vacuum.

"If one said that the Dow would drop 500 points in response to a collapse of the budget negotiations in Washington, then I think it would be an overreaction.

"On the other hand, if the Dow collapsed in the context of open economic warfare between the leading industrial nations, then I think you could look at a worldwide recession that is impending, and that would cause stocks to drop.

"So, if it were to happen again, I think it would be the result of an event that would have dire implications. I do believe in something like a rational expectations theory. The market does look at things and evaluates them before the next step is taken.

"There was a little bit of a problem before October 19. In 1987, it began to appear that foreigners were becoming reluctant to accumulate additional United States assets. There was an unusual accumulation of dollars in foreign central bank hands.

"If you try to maintain an exchange rate system, the truth of whether it's a sustainable system is revealed by the amount of central bank intervention necessary to preserve that structure. But by that criteria, 1987 showed that the dollar was essentially overvalued, and it couldn't be maintained at that level.

"There is also the ever-present possibility, and I think there is a distinct element of truth to it, that foreigners began to feel that they had enough U.S. dollars relative to their own currency. There is clear evidence that the Japanese institutional investors were getting very itchy about the exchange rate losses that they'd already taken and about any future ones that might be in store.

"That nervousness is the direct consequence of that ever-increasing trade deficit, which has to have as its counterpart a capital inflow.

"I think this reluctance is still present, and now it is particularly related to the decline of the dollar. The dollar has started moving downward as it was bound to. This event is one of the better things that I think has happened since October 19.

"You see, when Secretary Baker and the Germans were screaming at each other before October 19, in a way, it was a public expression. It was almost at the point where it had to break out into the open, the situation couldn't be handled behind closed doors anymore.

"Either the United States had to raise interest rates more than we were prepared to, or the Germans had to lower their interest rates more than they were prepared to, or the Germans had to run more of a budget deficit than they were prepared to, or else the exchange rate had to give ground.

"I'm not saying that the overvaluation of the dollar was the main cause of October 19, but it was a factor. The linkage was direct—through psychology it was indirect—to interest rates. The escalation of interest rates in the United States was bound to lead to a revaluation of stocks.

"Stocks compete with bonds. The higher the yield on bonds, the higher has to be the yield on stocks to be competitive. Stocks ran out of steam as our interest rates escalated. If you can get 10.5 percent on a 30-year government bond without any risk whatsoever, then where are the stocks?

"I'm forecasting slow growth, primarily because of consumer psychology. I don't know of any economist who had a positive forecast before and, on the basis of October 19 alone, changed it to a negative forecast.

"To find a period comparable to this one, I think that you most certainly would have to go back to the 1920s. Not since that time have you had such free international flow of finance and trade as now.

"But there are still differences. In those days, you still had the leading industrialized countries as the main engine of growth. Now, you find that the weight of the advance of worldwide economy has shifted to the Pacific rim. And that creates yet another facet.

"Nobody can come up with an exact analogy. Naturally, you do learn from history, and I think some reverses in the stock market have sometimes had real portent and sometimes they haven't. From the event alone, you can't be sure that anything major is happening in the real economy.

"Going back to 1929 or any of the other big stock market shakeouts, in almost every case, the market recovered until something else happened, such as bad economic news, which, in turn, might have been induced by the policy reaction, rather than by the original event alone.

"So what we are waiting for is some progress on the policy front. The first bit of progress has been made—that is, the exchange rates have again become more flexible.

"That step was essential.

"Whether the Washington people like the change in the exchange rate, or the people in Bonn or Tokyo like it, never mind. It just simply happened, because the market overwhelmed whatever official opinion to the contrary might still have existed.

"Since the exchange rates are moving in the right direction, and since there is some evidence that these new exchange rates might be more nearly feasible, perhaps this weakness is going to correct itself. The dollar might decline a little bit more, then it might be enough.

"The minute the U.S. trade deficit improves for three consecutive months, I predict that the dollar will strengthen.

"There are a number of silver linings to October 19.

"Number one, there has been no significant reaction in the real economy that would lead you to think that a recession or depression is actually coming up. There is no evidence whatever that people have reacted to the paper losses they've taken in a way that translates into anything that would have to lead to recession.

"Number two, by and large, the central banks have reacted in a responsive and responsible manner. Certainly, the fact that the Federal Reserve assured everybody of the availability of liquidity and made that happen was a very important stabilizer.

"Third, you had an international domestic policy off dead center. After October 19, you had an honest-to-goodness budget negotiation. As of December 1987, budget negotiations were concluded, but Congressional approval was still pending.

"In international finance, the exchanges are moving in accordance with normal market expectations, which tends to point toward eventual restoration of balance.

"So I think that there are a whole lot of silver linings, so many in fact that one could hope that October 19 was in fact isolated, a special event partly induced by technical factors internal to the market and that you have a better base on which to operate from now on."

Excerpts from an interview with Peter J. Solomon, vice chairman, Shearson Lehman Brothers, an investment bank in New York City.

"I didn't anticipate the date of the crash, its speed, or its severity. But there were signs that the market was on its way down.

"Initial public offerings, for example, had been sticky over the past six months. Retail stocks, as indicators of falling consumer spending, had turned down.

"From here on, I think investors can expect a highly volatile marketplace. We're in uncharted territory. It's not the same situation as it was in 1974 or 1981. These days, people don't have to wait in line for hours to buy gasoline, so they can still drive their cars to work. Also, we don't have double-digit inflation.

"Nevertheless, it's uncharted territory for a number of reasons.

"Levels of valuations in the market are still relatively high, but we don't know where they are going. The U.S. federal budget deficit and trade deficit are at historically high levels. So is our dependence on foreigners for direct investment and for the purchase of U.S. government securities.

"The Japanese, as well as other foreign investors, have propped up the American economy. In some ways, they're more important to the economy than American consumers are currently.

"The stock market crash has dramatically illustrated the new relationship between the foreign stock markets and the U.S. market. We've now seen globalization with a vengeance, the dark side of globalization. And once the situation started unwinding, it unwound quickly.

"Foreign investors have begun to pull money out of the United States, and the decline of the U.S. stock market has been to a very great extent the withdrawal of this liquidity.

"Foreign investors have been withdrawing capital for two reasons. First, they've been losing money, not only because of the market decline but because a declining dollar has eroded the value of their U.S. investments. Second, they've lost confidence in the ability of the United States to solve its economic problems.

"And it is foreign investors' lack of confidence in the dollar, and in Washington, that has been putting so much pressure on the market. It's an odd situation. You have Americans calm, foreigners upset, and Washington responding only to Americans.

"The public sector—meaning the Congress and the President—believe that the crash is something that only affected paper gains, let alone paper losses.

"And elected officials also believe that the stock market crash touched only Wall Street. This is a view that is shared by many Americans as you get away from Wall Street.

"They see it more as a media event—like the Contra hearings or an airplane crash—that will pass, and life will go on.

"This view creates an interesting paradox. To the extent that most Americans believe the postcrash economy is in good shape, the economy will stay better. In other words, Americans who believe that there really hasn't been a major problem will continue to spend and invest.

"But, at the same time, you want the public sector to believe that there *has* been a major problem, because you want them to address their overconsumption and overspending. But we know that the public sector won't get alarmed until pressure is put on them by the private sector. So this is the quandary we find ourselves in.

"For the long-run good of America, however, Washington must respond to the other members of G7 (the finance ministers of the United States, England, Canada, Germany, Japan, France, and Italy).

"The non-U.S. members of G7 have lost an enormous amount of confidence in Washington's ability to understand how to deal with what's going on. And they're being beggared by the fall of the dollar. But Washington isn't responding, and that is creating a problem.

"Six months before the crash, American public leaders could have gotten ahead of the curve by taking action to reduce deficit spending. Now, this failure to act has finally caught up with Washington. The world can see that the emperor has no clothes.

"Congress's and the administration's unwillingness to confront the deficit problem earlier has left them no choice but to deal with it during a time of greater uncertainty.

"So what needs to be done?

"The Fed must be extraordinarily skillful at following a monetary policy that counterbalances a tighter fiscal policy but that does not fan inflationary fears. The administration and the Congress must continue to jawbone other G7 members to stimulate their economies, while making the American people feel that everything's going to be okay.

"As far as the market goes, I do think we're in a bear market—and probably will stay in one through 1988 at least.

"I also feel any new president has about three months to go to the public and say, 'We've got to take X billion dollars out of the budget deficit to get this situation straightened out.'

"Taking such an action may cause a recession in his first year in office. But every president survives a recession in his first year, including Ronald Reagan. Presidents make their mistake in trying to keep the economy going. A recession usually occurs in their third year, and they don't get reelected in the fourth.

"We must all realize that by living off deficits, we're condemning our children to a standard of living lower than our own. Every day we rely on other people to supply the capital to finance our indebtedness, we put a greater burden on someone else, someone younger, to pay it back.

"Americans spend an awful lot of time worrying about their children's welfare—feeding them, educating them, clothing them. But as long as citizens don't put pressure on their government to get these things in hand, they're just transferring wealth from their children to foreigners.

"That's a much more severe problem than worrying whether

the Dow is at 2700 or 2200 or 1800. Stocks fluctuate, but the transfer of our wealth just goes on.

"What are the lessons to be learned from the market collapse?

"There is a silver lining to the stock market crash. It may force us to come to terms with our economic problems—to strike a better balance between consumption and saving and investment. Remember, the deficits are not the cause of this imbalance; they are evidence of it.

"We have to remember that stocks do fluctuate and that every market ends—sometimes with a bang and sometimes with a whimper. This market ended with a bang, but it had also made just as much noise on its way up.

"In these times, you must take a Chinese point of view, which says that life is long, and that you keep striving to make it better. And you hope that, someday, it will be better."

Excerpts from an interview with David A. Wyss, chief financial economist for Data Resources in Lexington, Massachusetts.

"The market dropped because it went so high, and people eventually came to the realization that it was overvalued. Everybody tried to get out at once, and they couldn't. But what investors want to know is, what lies ahead?

"The inflation outlook really hasn't changed much.

"We're expecting a little more than 4.5 percent in 1988—a little less than that in the first half, a little more in the second half. In my opinion, the inflation rate depends more on what happens in the Persian Gulf than what happens to the economy.

"GNP during the first half should grow about 0.8 percent. During the second half, about 1.8 percent. I think, and those numbers indicate, that we're going to see a slowdown, but no recession in 1988—that is, if we don't make too many mistakes.

"But to avoid a recession we need four events to occur. Number one, we need a significant plan to cut the federal budget deficit.

"Number two, we need to lower interest rates, not only in the United States but worldwide, to offset the impact of lower stock prices.

"Number three, the stock market must stabilize at a reasonable level, so that we don't continue to slice off household wealth.

"And, number four, we need to make sure we don't do anything too stupid to destroy international cooperation and slow the flow of dollars coming in from foreign investors.

"If the dollar flow into the United States were to slow, the dollar would go through the floor, and U.S. interest rates would go through the ceiling. We've become dependent on that foreign capital. It's financing a good portion of our federal deficit.

"Fortunately, I don't think that foreign investors are likely to stop investing here. One reason is that the Japanese investor knows that there is no better place to put money right now. We've survived two-and-a-half years of very sharp declines in the value of the dollar without the Japanese investor panicking, and I don't see any signs that he's suddenly going to begin to run.

"The one danger to my mind is the trade bill. It would raise a lot of doubts in Japanese investors' minds. I'm pretty sure that President Reagan would veto it, but we're going to have another president in a year, and who knows what he's going to do?

"The markets may start worrying about that ahead of time, because the trade bill sends a signal to the Japanese that we don't want them."

Part II

DAMAGE CONTROL

2

FEELING FLUSH
The Outlook for Cash and Cash Equivalents

Cash is the medium that lets you hold onto your money while all about you people are losing theirs. And that's why more people have been jumping on the cash bandwagon.

Cash and cash equivalents—short-term certificates of deposit, money-market accounts, and money-market funds—offer investors safety and steady returns.

In the wake of the market crash, how far from the cash shelter should you venture? We turned to four respected money mavens for the answers. Their names are:

- Paul A. Bauer, publisher of two newsletters—*Tiered Rate Watch* and *Jumbo Rate News*—that monitor certificate of deposit (CD) rates nationwide. His company, Bauer Communications Inc., is based in Coral Gables, Florida.
- William E. Donoghue, bestselling financial author, syndicated columnist, and publisher of *Donoghue's Moneyletter*. Among his titles: *The Complete Money Market Guide*, *The No-Load Mutual Fund Guide*, and *The Guide to Finding Money to Invest*. His company is based in Holliston, Massachusetts.

- Thomas Heagy, executive vice president of the Exchange National Bank, an institution which is headquartered in Chicago.
- Thomas J. Wageman, chairman, president, and chief executive officer of Sunbelt Savings Association in Dallas. Sunbelt is the country's fifth largest savings & loan.

Here's what these experts had to say.

Do you think anything has changed after the crash? Should people do anything differently?

Bauer: "There's a lot of money coming into the money market. That's why the rates are staying artificially down right now. I think they'll go up. It's still a buyer's market as far as credit goes. It's going to start to pick up again."

Wageman: "It's almost as if people have to relearn the lessons of the Depression. How can you beat compound interest?

"The average American had no business in the stock market. It's a trader's market. The only people who made money were the people who traded every day.

"The fact is, nobody can explain why the market collapsed. And if you can't explain the collapse, you can't explain why the market was as high as it was.

"And if you don't understand that, why were you in the market to start with?"

How much money would you have in cash right now?

Bauer: "I have a bias. I'd stay liquid. But I don't see a bottom side on interest rates right now. I don't think they're going to drop. So the only thing that can happen to you is they're going to go up.

"I think that too many people are talking about the psychology of the market and comparing it to 1929. There's nothing really positive that would lead me to believe there's going to be a recovery. I'm a real bear on this. And CD rates are fine."

Donoghue: "If I were a conservative investor, I would have a substantial amount in money funds—maybe 70 percent."

Heagy: "I think that cash equivalents should be a permanent part of anyone's portfolio. Not just to the extent needed for liquidity, but for diversification.

"People should not be going into cash equivalents now just because they were scared of the collapse in the stock market, with the idea that they are then going to pull out their money and go back into the stock market when they think they can get rich again.

"Any prudent investor has to be diversified. And a diversified portfolio should include a significant amount of cash-equivalent investments."

How significant in your view?

Heagy: "I would say 20 percent."

What's the best way to evaluate cash equivalents?

Heagy: "The most important part of evaluating a cash-equivalent investment is to make sure that it really *is* cash equivalent.

"For example, a lot of people bought Ginnie Mae mutual funds under the mistaken assumption that those were cash equivalents. And, while they were backed by U.S. government-guaranteed bonds and were liquid, you could get your money out only at the market price of the bonds.

"So a lot of people invested in those funds and ended up losing money. Not to criticize Ginnie Maes as an investment, but they're just not a cash equivalent.

"What's most important, then, is that you can get at your money, that you have no credit risk, and that you have no market-valuation risk. You want to know that you can get out what you put in plus your interest. And those investments really boil down to two alternatives: bank deposits and money-market mutual funds."

Why are money-market funds a good place to park your cash now?

Donoghue: "The obvious way to avoid crashes is not to be in a market that crashes. The money market certainly has gone through all the strains one can imagine over the last decade, and money-market mutual funds have proven their ability to be safe harbors in times of stress."

Don't you have a small chance of losing money?

Donoghue: "No one has ever lost money in a money fund. No money fund has ever invested in anything that did not pay off at maturity. And, through the whole time, money funds have paid competitive money-market rates.

"In fact, they're arguably better and safer than bank deposits. Certainly for amounts of more than $100,000, I'd rather be in a money fund than in a bank."

Why?

Donoghue: "True, bank deposits are insured. But if you look at the spread between bank money-market deposit accounts and money funds, it's currently about 80 basis points. That's very expensive insurance, particularly if you're living off the money from your money-market investments."

What are the two types of money-market funds?

Heagy: "You have a choice of taxable and tax-free."

Which investors should opt for tax-free funds?

Heagy: "Only people in the highest bracket under the new tax law—meaning people in the 28-percent bracket in 1988—would want to consider the tax-exempt funds."

How do tax-free money funds work?

Donoghue: "They invest in short-term obligations of tax-exempt authorities and municipalities. Some of these funds are available in double- or triple-tax-free forms.

"For example, some companies have funds for, say, New York State and New York City—wherever there's enough quality investments available and there's a large enough market for them. And that's in those states where there are high taxes."

Aren't there different types of taxable funds?

Donoghue: "There are three types of taxable funds.

"One is the government-only money fund that invests 100 percent in U.S. government securities—Treasury bills and repurchase agreements secured by Treasury bills. Other government funds also invest in the securities of government agencies.

"More broadly based funds invest in bank CDs, commercial paper, and other types of investments. These funds normally provide a higher rate of return."

Is there any difference in safety?

Heagy: "There is a real, but very, very small difference in credit risk. But any well-run corporate fund—one that invests in CDs and commercial paper—will be very well diversified and carry extremely low risk. It's similar to buying a Triple A bond. There's very little risk. But it's still not government backed."

Which investors should opt for government funds?

Heagy: "It's really a subjective judgment, whether or not the slightly higher yield on the corporate money-market fund is worth the slight additional risk."

What's the difference between the rates each pays?

Donoghue: "Treasury-only funds usually have a lesser yield—the average 30-day yield is 5.85 percent. Those that invest in the securities of government agencies average about 6.25 percent. So the overall average for government funds is about 6.05 percent.

"The overall return on nongovernment money funds is around 6.5 percent. The recent 30-day average yield is 6.52 percent."

Heagy: "The spread between government and nongovernment funds varies a great deal. Right now, it's probably higher than normal, because there's been a flight to quality. The rates on Treasury bills have been driven down relative to other interest rates."

What rates do these funds currently pay?

Heagy: "For government funds, you can find rates ranging anywhere from 5.5 percent to 6.5 percent. Depending on the specific investments a fund has made, its yield may be above or below average for one month and then do the opposite the next month."

Donoghue: "The yield right now on nongovernment funds is about 6.5 percent or 7 percent. If we have inflation and we see interest rates rising, money funds will pay a higher and higher return as market rates go up. If interest rates fall, of course, their yield will fall. But their price-per-share will never vary, and that's really the key."

Should investors keep switching from one fund to another to get the best rates?

Heagy: "For anyone other than people who have invested extremely large amounts, it does not make sense to try to switch back and forth."

Let's go back to the safety issue. Are all money-market funds equally safe?

Donoghue: "History tells us that all money funds are equal in safety. But, in recent crashes, we've seen that what we thought was safe was not really safe at all."

Here's the question point blank. Do you think there is at least some risk in investing in money-market funds?

Donoghue: "Let's look where there may be risk.

"There is a story that I see frequently about a fund called First Multifund for Daily Income in which people lost 7 percent of their money. But First Multifund wasn't a money-market fund at all. It was impersonating a money fund.

"It had an average maturity of 650 days. That's not a money fund. That's a short-term bond fund no matter what you call it."

How can investors avoid situations like this one?

Donoghue: "Realize that if there might be any risk in a money fund, it would be in a fund—regardless of its portfolio—that had a long average maturity.

"Certainly, in times of stress in the marketplace where interest rates could reverse direction quickly, I would want to be in a fund with a less-than-60-day average maturity. But most funds are usually in the 30- to 50-day average-maturity range.

"I would also avoid, as a money-market fund, one fund that has been getting a lot of publicity lately and is clearly *not* a money fund. It's called Money Market Plus and is put out by Neuberger and Berman. It can have an average maturity of 360 days, which is extremely long. But in a declining interest-rate market, it would have a little higher rate of return.

"So that's one superprecaution. There's no evidence of anyone losing money—that's simply a place where you *might* have a small problem.

"I would describe the risk as probably a one-in-a-thousand chance you might lose 1 percent and a 50-percent chance you'd get it back. That's not a risk worth worrying about."

Any other precautions an investor should take?

Heagy: "Certainly one is better off going with one of the larger companies, such as Kemper, Fidelity, or Dreyfus."

Donoghue: "I would tend to avoid smaller funds, those with less than $100 million in assets, because they have less seasoned management. In the table we publish in the newspapers (including the *Wall Street Journal*), all those funds are more than $100 million in assets. These tables appear in most newspapers on Mondays or Fridays."

Besides safety and yield, what do investors get out of a money fund?

Donoghue: "You get liquidity, and you get the absence of hidden service charges, which can be significant if you're with a bank. And then, of course, you have free checking, and, in some cases, unlimited checking, which can be very attractive."

Any other tips on money funds?

Donoghue: "Stock-market investors may want to keep their money in a money fund run by the fund family in which they want to invest.

"Or if they want to choose among families, they might consider a Schwab One account, which uses the Kemper money-market fund, which, incidentally, is a super money fund. They've been in the top ten since God created money funds.

"Schwab has a mutual-fund marketplace where you can buy no-load mutual funds. They charge a transaction fee. But the account conveniently allows you to move from one fund in one family to another fund in another family."

Would you choose money funds now, over, say short-term CDs?

Donoghue: "I would prefer to be in money-market funds at this point, simply because there is no current consensus on what the easy answer is. There's good reason to sit by the wayside and watch.

"The risk of another downside decline is as great as an immediate rally. And I'd rather miss some opportunities than get zapped again."

What's the advantage of a bank money-market account—or, indeed, any bank deposit?

Heagy: "As long as you invest $100,000 or less, your money is fully guaranteed by the Federal Deposit Insurance Corporation (FDIC), which is backed by the full faith and credit of the U.S. government."

What precisely is a bank money-market account?

Heagy: "A money-market account at a bank is a deposit account. If you have a money-market account, it means the bank owes you money.

"Your money goes into the bank's general pool of funds, which is used to buy government bonds and municipal bonds, to make loans, and so forth."

And how does a money-market account differ from a money-market mutual fund?

Heagy: "In a money-market fund, you participate in whatever pool of investments the fund makes. The fund sponsor has no absolute liability to pay you back X dollars at X point in time. With a bank deposit, the performance of the assets that the bank purchases does not affect your rate of return.

"The bank contractually obligates itself to pay you a certain rate and to return your principal on demand. So if the bank ends up making bad loans, it won't affect you. The bank has its own reserves and its own capital. And even if the bank went under, the FDIC would step in and take over the responsibility."

What about rates?

Heagy: "The spread on rates that are available on bank money-market accounts is really astounding. For example, right now there are people offering money-market accounts with yields ranging all the way from 5 percent and up."

Does the FDIC guarantee interest as well as principal?

Heagy: "It guarantees interest as well. However, there is one caveat. The guarantee is $100,000, inclusive of interest and principal.

"So if, for example, you had a $100,000 CD and were owed $5,000 in interest, your FDIC insurance would cover only the $100,000. But if you had a $90,000 CD and $5,000 interest due, it would cover the full $95,000.

"However, with most bank failures, the banks are taken over in such a way that even those depositors with more than $100,000 get out whole."

In the case of a bank failure, is there much of a wait before you can get at your money?

Heagy: "No. I don't want to say there have been no exceptions. But I can't think of any situation where a bank closure has caused a delay in payment.

"Here's why. Generally what happens is on, say, Thursday night the bank of X closes down. Overnight, they change the sign on the window, and the next day the bank opens for business as usual. The only thing is, it's a different bank.

"So there's really no inconvenience at all. You usually don't even have to bother filing claims."

Let's talk about money-market accounts offered by credit unions and savings and loans. Is there a difference in rates?

Heagy: "There are a lot of differences among different institutions. As a rule, savings and loans pay slightly higher rates than do banks.

"And there are 2 reasons. One is that there are many more cases in the savings and loan industry where the regulators have limited themselves to the statutory insurance, and people with over $100,000 have had to take a loss.

"Second, there are far more cases in the savings and loan industry where someone has had to wait for his or her money. These accounts are backed by the Federal Savings and Loan Insurance Corporation (FSLIC). Principal and interest are insured up to $100,000.

"In most cases, the system has worked the way I described. On one day, the institution is one savings and loan. On the next day, it's another.

"But there have been quite a few cases where the S&Ls have not been able to do that, where people had to file claims, and, in some cases, had some significant delay. But as long as you have less than $100,000, there is no risk ultimately, other than the possibility of delay."

What about Treasuries?

Heagy: "I would not recommend short-term Treasuries. First, the yield is very poor. Right now, a three-month Treasury gives you a rate of less than 6 percent. You also have a transaction cost when you buy a Treasury bill. And if you want to sell it before maturity, you have a transaction cost then as well."

What are these transaction costs?

Heagy: "Transaction costs are a function of the size of your purchase. Many people buy odd lots. And here the transaction cost—if you bought a Treasury and later sold it before maturity—could lower your yield 25 basis points or more.

"If you're confident that you can wait until maturity to cash out, you're better off buying a CD. And if you're not sure, you're better off being in a money-market account. There are times when this rule isn't true. But, right now, the spread between Treasury bills and CDs is unusually wide."

What are the advantages and disadvantages of CDs?

Heagy: "The advantage is that you can get somewhat higher rates. For example, with a six-month CD, which is probably the most popular single maturity, you can easily get a 7 percent return.

"The disadvantage, of course, is that if you need the money before the end of the six months, you have to pay an early withdrawal penalty. But as long as you can count on not needing your money, you have total safety and a higher yield."

Is demand for three-month CDs on the rise?

Heagy: "We've seen some demand for them. Nobody used to buy them. They're a compromise between the traditional six-month CD and a money-market account. People who want to be liquid but want a little better yield than they can get in a money-market account like them."

What are the new bull and bear CDs?

Heagy: "Those are bundled products. You're buying a CD, and you're also buying a stock-index option. The bank lowers the rate on the CD and uses the difference to purchase the option.

"By the way, the price of the option is much higher now than when they first started selling these CDs. The market has realized that the stock market is very volatile. So the price of the option has gotten very high."

How do these CDs work?

Heagy: "Say you buy a six-month CD that pays no interest, but you get 60 percent of the increase in the S&P 500. The bank takes your money and invests most of it. But it takes part of it and buys a call option with a six-month maturity on the S&P 500.

"At the end of the six months, the bank liquidates the option. If the S&P 500 had gone up, there would be a profit and that profit would go to the customer.

"If the S&P 500 had not gone up, the customer would get nothing except the return of his or her principal. The interest that the bank would have paid on the CD covers the cost of buying the option."

What's the effect on the customer of the option price having gone up?

Heagy: "Say before October 19, you bought a six-month CD with zero interest and got 75 percent of any rise in the S&P 500. With the same CD today, you'd probably get only 55 percent of the rise in the S&P 500 and still no interest. So you're getting less bang for your buck."

Why have the option writers boosted the price?

Heagy: "There were quite a few people who were very active in the business of writing put options who literally went bankrupt on October 19.

"And that's one of the reasons why people are less eager to write them. And if they're going to do it, they're going to charge a lot more."

What do you think of these bull and bear CDs—and other more exotic products? Do you think they are good investments?

Heagy: "I think they are good investments for people who do not have stock portfolios and would like to participate in what they and I hope will be a new bull market, without getting into stocks directly. Someone who has a stock portfolio does not benefit very much by buying the CDs, because they're already investing in that market in a much more cost-effective way.

"For someone who does not have the ability to trade in options on listed exchanges, these CDs are really the only way that you can make that kind of investment—that is, bet on the rise or fall in the stock market without risking a great deal of money. You're risking only your interest, not your principal."

Bauer: "I think anything other than a plain vanilla certificate is misleading. They've already pulled most of the bear and bull CDs off the market.

"With a lot of the other exotic CDs, they give you the loss leader—the first three months is a great rate, then it drops back to a little bit better than passbook rate.

"If you want to gamble, bet on whether the Dolphins are going to win by 14 points. Otherwise, just stay with a plain vanilla certificate where you know what the yield is over your term."

When do short-term CDs make sense and when do longer-term CDs (which of course aren't really cash equivalents) make sense?

Donoghue: "If you think interest rates are going to fall further, then you might want to go into longer-term CDs. If you think interest rates are likely to rise, then shorter-term CDs make sense."

Are there any disadvantages to getting the highest rate CDs by buying them through the mail across state lines?

Heagy: "I would recommend that people not buy CDs that are not issued by institutions in their own locale. You can do computer searches and find the highest rate CD anywhere in the country. But when maturity time comes, it can be very inconvenient if you can't actually go to the institution yourself, particularly in case of a default.

"I suggest people just telephone the largest 12 banks and savings and loans in their area and check the rates. If you do go out of state, you definitely want to do everything through registered mail."

Donoghue: "I would look in *Barron's* every week and get the highest yielding CDs in the country. If they're federally insured, you're safe. But I would never buy a CD that matured at more than $100,000. That's a reasonable precaution.

"I would also make sure that I had good documentation to present to the FDIC if the bank fails. Before I bought the CD, I would get a preassigned account number over the phone. If they wouldn't give me the number, I wouldn't send the check.

"On the back of my check, I'd put 'for deposit only' to that preassigned number. This procedure reduces the risk of an accounting error and gives you a piece of paper to use as evidence in case of default."

Bauer: "I see no disadvantage to buying CDs out of state. I don't see any problem with losing money, even in a troubled institution. People just have to concern themselves with *never* going over $100,000, including interest, in any institution.

"But I also tell people to avoid the less-than-creditworthy institutions, because the only place that you can really distinguish a difference in rates is in the jumbo market. Consumers can find as good a rate in a creditworthy institution as they can in the other ones."

How do you determine if an institution is creditworthy?

Bauer: "At *Tiered Rate Watch*, we survey each month between 500 and 600 banks and thrifts that we consider creditworthy.

"To qualify, the institutions must have a capital ratio exceeding three percent, not have delinquencies in excess of 200 percent of net worth, and not have a quarterly loss that, when annualized, exceeds 10 percent of net worth.

"Basically we want to know that they're sound, and they're going to be around in ten or twenty years."

What are CD rates right now? What should investors look for in a CD?

Bauer: "You can get a yield even on a short-term CD of around 9 percent. But different minimum amounts produce different results, even with the same institution.

"I also see money-market accounts yielding in excess of 8 percent. And if you want to get into yields of 9 percent you can get a three-year, even a two-year CD, yielding 9.14.

"But in this market I wouldn't tell anybody to go long. I'd tell them to stay short."

What's the longest term you'd recommend?

Bauer: "Six months to a year. The best you're going to do for a year, as of our last survey, is 8.9 percent. And the best money market account is 9.0 percent."

What should people do who do want to buy a longer-term CD?

Donoghue: "If you think interest rates are going to fall, I would suggest you be even more aggressive than just buying a year's CD or an 18-month CD. You may want to buy a 5- or 10-year CD.

"If you are going to do that, the way to get a competitive yield is to buy through Merrill Lynch. Even if you can get a higher return, never buy a long-term CD directly.

"Here's why. Merrill Lynch will maintain a secondary market. You may want to buy a 10-year CD and hold it for a year. If interest rates have gone down, you can sell it back to Merrill Lynch for a profit. If interest rates have gone up, your penalty will probably be less than the early withdrawal penalty that you get from your bank."

Bauer: "I tell our subscribers that if they're going to go long, make sure to get a written agreement with the institution stating that it will lend them their money back at 1.5 to 2 points above what they're receiving. This is a common procedure.

"Say you get a CD that's paying 8.5 percent. And the bank agrees to lend it back to you at 10.5 percent. If rates go through the roof, you can then reinvest the same funds somewhere else at 12 percent or 13 percent."

What about jumbos?

Bauer: "The jumbos—$98,000—are hot money. And over the past two years, there's been a differential of around 1.5 percent between troubled institutions and creditworthy ones.

"We recommend to professional managers that they stay away from troubled institutions, even though they've got nothing to lose. And a lot of them agree. They say, 'I don't even want the paperwork that goes into getting my money back. I don't want my board to know that I was that hot for a rate that I invested in somebody that went belly-up.' "

What other advice do you have for people looking for CDs right now?

Bauer: "I tell subscribers that if it means that much to them to pick up a quarter point on $50,000, it's their business. But my contention is stay with the creditworthy institutions, get yourself a good rate, lock it in, and sleep at night."

What's wrong with squeezing out that last dollar?

Bauer: "People don't realize that the contract with the institution is good only as long as the institution exists.

"So if your CD is transferred to a new institution and that institution doesn't want to meet the contract, it can convert your CD to a 5.5 percent money-market account. Now, you have to shop around and find someone else who's going to pay you a reasonable rate.

"If interest rates are down, you can come up short.

"Say a year ago you took out a three-year CD that paid 10 percent. You get your 10 percent for a year, and the bank goes under.

"Now you're stuck with 5.5 percent, and you have to shop around. You may get only 8 percent now. You would have been better off to take a quarter point less with an institution that could honor its commitment."

HIGHEST YIELDS

Top 10 Money-Market Accounts

INSTITUTION	*MINIMUM ($)*	*RATE (%)*	*YIELD (%)*
First Deposit National Bank, Tilton, NH	5,000	8.62	9.00
Far Western Bank, Tustin, CA	25,000	8.09	8.30
Mission S&L Assn, Riverside, CA	50,000	7.25	7.52
New England FSB, Wellesley, MA	2,500	7.23	7.50
TCF Banc Savings, Houston, TX	2,500	7.50	7.50
Seaboard Savings, Stuart, FL	50,000	7.22	7.50
Penn Savings Bank, Reading, PA	25,000	7.23	7.50
Coastal Banc Savings, Houston, TX	2,500	7.40	7.40
So. Financial Fed S&L, Herndon, VA	10,000	7.10	7.35
Far West S&L, Los Angeles, CA	5,000	7.02	7.28

Top 10 Three-Month CDs

INSTITUTION	*MINIMUM ($)*	*RATE (%)*	*YIELD (%)*
TCF Banc Savings, Houston, TX	1,000	8.30	8.55
Westcoast S&L, Pac. Palisades, CA	500	8.00	8.32
Gold River, FSB, Fair Oaks, CA	50,000	8.25	8.25
Gold River, FSB, Fair Oaks, CA	500	7.75	8.06
Far Western Bank, Tustin, CA	10,000	7.75	8.03
Skylake State Bank, North Miami Beach, FL	25,000	8.00	8.00
Girad Savings Bank, San Diego, CA	50,000	8.00	8.00
Girad Savings Bank, San Diego, CA	20,000	7.65	7.95
Malaga S&L, Palos Ver. Est, CA	50,000	7.63	7.92
Girad Savings Bank, San Diego, CA	10,000	7.60	7.90

Top 10 Six-Month CDs

INSTITUTION	*MINIMUM ($)*	*RATE (%)*	*YIELD (%)*
Capital Bank & Trust, Boston, MA	1,000	8.30	8.62
Gold River, FSB, Fair Oaks, CA	50,000	8.45	8.45
New England FSB, Wellesley, MA	5,000	8.07	8.40
Westcoast S&L, Pac. Palisades, CA	500	8.05	8.38
First Commercial S&L, Phoenix, AZ	10,000	8.10	8.35
Gold River, FSB, Fair Oaks, CA	500	8.00	8.30
La Jolla Savings Bank, La Jolla, CA	10,000	8.25	8.25
Westside S&L, Los Angeles, CA	50,000	8.25	8.25
Guaranty First Bank, Waltham, MA	1,000	8.00	8.24
Financial Savings SA, Dallas, TX	25,000	7.85	8.20

Top 10 One-Year CDs

INSTITUTION	*MINIMUM ($)*	*RATE (%)*	*YIELD (%)*
New England FSB, Wellesley, MA	5,000	8.53	8.90
First Commercial S&L, Phoenix, AZ	10,000	8.50	8.77
Malibu S&L, Fountain Valley, CA	1,000	8.25	8.72
TCF Banc Savings, Houston, TX	1,000	8.35	8.61
Vista Federal, SB, Reston, VA	1,000	8.25	8.60
Gold River, FSB, Fair Oaks, CA	50,000	8.60	8.60
Guaranty First Bank, Waltham, MA	1,000	8.30	8.56
Financial Savings SA, Dallas, TX	25,000	8.15	8.52
Home Owners Fed S&L, Burlington, MA	500	8.15	8.52
Seaboard Savings, Stuart, FL	1,000	8.14	8.50

Top 5 Two-Year CDs

INSTITUTION	*MINIMUM ($)*	*RATE (%)*	*YIELD (%)*
Vista Federal, SB, Reston, VA	1,000	8.75	9.14
Washington SB, Waldorf, MD	1,000	8.75	9.04
First Commercial S&L, Phoenix, AZ	10,000	8.75	9.04
New England FSB, Wellesley, MA	5,000	8.62	9.00
Americity FSB, Dallas, TX	1,000	8.55	8.89

Top 5 Three-Year CDs

INSTITUTION	*MINIMUM ($)*	*RATE (%)*	*YIELD (%)*
Vista Federal, SB, Reston, VA	1,000	9.00	9.42
First Commercial S&L, Phoenix, AZ	10,000	9.00	9.31
Second National Fed S&L, Salisbury, MD	1,000	9.00	9.31
Seaboard Savings, Stuart, FL	1,000	8.82	9.25
Americity FSB, Dallas, TX	1,000	8.80	9.16

Top 5 Five-Year CDs

INSTITUTION	*MINIMUM ($)*	*RATE (%)*	*YIELD (%)*
USA Savings, Rockville, MD	25,000	10.15	10.15
Washington SB, Waldorf, MD	1,000	9.75	10.11
Far Western Bank, Tustin, CA	10,000	9.60	10.03
Second National Fed S&L, Salisbury, MD	1,000	9.50	9.84
Vista Federal, SB, Reston, VA	1,000	9.25	9.69

Source: *Tiered Rate Watch*, the highest yields from federally insured, creditworthy banks and thrifts, Coral Gables, FL

Top Performing Government-Only Money Funds

FUND	*YIELD (%)*
CMA Government Securities	7.19
Merrill Lynch USA Government Reserve	7.14
Massachusetts Cash Management Trust	7.05
The Galaxy Funds Government Fund	6.91
HighMark U.S. Government Obligations	6.89
Kemper Government Money Market	6.89
Vanguard Money Market Reserve	6.86
Monitor U.S. Government Money Market	6.83
Cardinal Government Securities	6.78
Merrill Lynch Government A	6.77

Top Performing General-Purpose Money Funds

FUND	*YIELD (%)*
CMA Money Fund	7.42
Merrill Lynch Ready	7.41
Summitt Cash Reserves	7.35
Flex-Fund Money Market Fund	7.21
Alger Money Market Portfolio	7.19
Vanguard Money Market Reserve Prime	7.17
HighMark Dividend Obligation Fund	7.08
Kemper Money Market	7.05
Trinity Liquid Assets Trust	7.04
Monitor Money Market Fund	7.02
The Galaxy Funds Money Market	7.02

Top Performing Tax-Free Money Funds

FUND	*YIELD (%)*
Colonial Tax-Exempt Money Market Trust	5.45
Strong Tax-Free Money Market	5.14
Shearson/Provident Muni Cash	5.03
Horizon Tax-Exempt Money Fund	5.02
Lazard Freres Institutional Trust	4.97
Shearson/Provident Muni Fund	4.97
Shearson/Provident Muni for California	4.95
USAA Tax-Exempt Money Market Fund	4.92
Nuveen Tax-Exempt Money Market Fund	4.91
Vanguard Municipal Bond Money Market	4.90

Source: *Donoghue's Money Fund Report*, Holliston, Massachusetts. All funds ranked by October 1987 monthly yield.

3

SOLID AS A ROCK?
The Outlook for Fixed-Income Instruments

Extra cautious investors have traditionally favored bonds over stocks. A bit boring, perhaps, but bonds were safe.

Bondholders, for instance, knew that their annual income from their investment wouldn't vary. And their earnings didn't depend on the vagaries of profits or the unpredictable whims of corporate directors making dividend decisions.

Bondholders knew—to the dollar—what their investments would be worth at maturity. After all, the value was printed right there on the certificate.

And while stock prices might dip and soar, the value of bonds on the secondary market changed—but only slowly and then not by much.

Alas, those were the good old days.

Now, there's almost as much excitement in managing a bond portfolio as there is in trading stocks. Most, but not quite all, of the certainties have disappeared. And bonds, in the current environment, are no longer the favorite vehicle of the faint of heart.

In fact, before stocks took their spectacular nosedive, the bond market took its own plunge. From April to September

1987, bonds—depending on the type—lost from 10 percent to 25 percent of their value.

Of course, bonds are still worthwhile investments. And most financial advisers recommend that investors make them part of their portfolios. But investing well in the bond market now demands the same kinds of evaluative skills and attention to timing as investing in the equity market.

What happens to the bond market depends on what happens to interest rates. And we all know that interest rates are anything but stable.

When interest rates rise, bondholders can expect a reduction in the value of their portfolios. When rates fall, the value of their bonds rise.

But what factors influence interest rates? When they rise, or fall, are all bonds affected equally? What bonds are a good buy now? Which should you avoid? These are just a few of the questions we put to our panel of experts. We include their answers in this chapter.

Our fixed-income experts range from executives of top financial services firms to managers of some of the nation's largest bond funds and bond portfolios. Their names:

- Peter Anderson, senior vice president and director of equity investments for IDS Financial Services, a subsidiary of American Express in Minneapolis, Minnesota.
- Ted Busboom, senior vice president and manager of fixed-income investments for IDS.
- William E. Donoghue, bestselling financial author, syndicated columnist, and publisher of *Donoghue's Moneyletter*. Among his titles: *The Complete Money Market Guide*, *The No-Load Mutual Fund Guide*, and *The Guide to Finding Money to Invest*. The company is based in Holliston, Massachusetts.
- Jeremy G. Duffield, senior vice president for The Vanguard Group of Investment Companies in Valley Forge, Pennsylvania.

- Jean-Marie Eveillard, portfolio manager for the Sogen International Fund, a top-performing mutual fund, based in New York City.
- Monte J. Gordon, vice president and director of research for Dreyfus Corp. in New York City. Gordon is also a regular on public television's "Wall Street Week."
- Michael S. Gray, vice president and group leader of the taxable bond division for giant Fidelity Investments in Boston.
- C. Bruce Johnstone, managing director of Boston-based Fidelity Investments and portfolio manager of Fidelity's Equity Income Fund. He also serves as senior vice president and income-growth group leader for Fidelity Management and Research, a subsidiary of Fidelity Investments.
- Nita Kincaid, senior vice president for retail services for Fidelity Investments.
- Douglas M. Loudon, managing director for Scudder, Stevens & Clark, which has its headquarters in New York City.
- John D. Markese, vice president and research director for the American Association of Individual Investors, which is based in Chicago.
- Paul E. Suckow, executive vice president and director of fixed-income securities for Oppenheimer Management in New York City.
- Spike Thorne, managing director and bond portfolio manager for Scudder, Stevens & Clark.
- David Wyss, chief financial economist for Data Resources, a subsidiary of McGraw-Hill, which has its headquarters in Lexington, Massachusetts.

Here's what our experts had to say.

The bond market crashed first, right?

Loudon: "Yes. Interest rates, of course, had risen tremendously from the end of March to the end of September. In fact, that was actually one of the worst bear markets for bonds that we ever had in a six-month period. Yet, you read almost nothing about it."

So let's recap what's happened.

Gray: "For the first nine-and-one-half months of the year, the stock market significantly outperformed the bond market. The stock averages were up, say, 35 percent until the middle of October, and total return for bonds was down about 5 percent.

"So you had stocks outperforming bonds by about 40 percent for the first nine-and-one-half months of the year. When the market crashed, that relationship reversed.

"Bonds then started outperforming stocks."

So investors shifted from stocks to bonds?

Gray: "A lot of people started hating stocks and buying bonds. They were buying bonds, because they thought interest rates would decline. They thought the market crash was a sign that the economy was heading into a recession. And, with recessions, interest rates usually fall.

"But there was another factor in the switch from stocks to bonds. Bond yields had risen to about 10 percent. They were trading at roughly 10.25 to 10.50 percent. So, suddenly, bonds looked attractive to people who wanted to lock in a good return for a period of time."

Did the collapse of the stock and bond markets surprise you?

Busboom: "Not really. We're in a kind of future-shock environment where the minute you think of something, it happens."

How do investors respond in times like these?

Busboom: "People become more cautious. For example, the assets in cash-management accounts have grown steadily since the stock-market crash."

How do professionals respond?

Gray: "We always change our strategies when the market environment changes. And this certainly was viewed as a significant change in the market.

"We were in a defensive mode prior to the crash—that is, we were in shorter-term securities. But when we recognized that the bond market was going to do better and rates were going to decline, we became less defensive and more aggressive and bought longer-term securities."

When investors shifted from stocks to bonds, what kinds of bonds did they opt for?

Gray: "Whenever there is a financial crisis—and the crash of the stock market was certainly a financial crisis—there's a flight to quality. That means investors usually buy the highest quality issues, and those are U.S. Treasuries.

"Treasuries have performed the best in the bond market rally. They're the easiest to get into and the most liquid. So that's what people are buying.

"People are also moving into other high-quality investments, such as mortgage-backed securities. Next in line are high-grade corporate bonds. The junks tended to underperform over the past months. Most of the new money was concentrated in the high-quality, liquid, fixed-income securities."

So are bonds a better buy than stocks now?

Thorne: "When you look at bonds against the background of history, when you look at the long-term, high-quality stream of income you receive after inflation, bonds are cheap now. The stock market, in contrast, is fairly valued, but it is not cheap."

Gray: "I can't really say whether bonds are a better buy than stocks. Some people would argue they are. But you could make an equally good argument that they are not.

"Most financial advisers tell investors that the key is to diversify your assets. You should not put all your eggs in one basket. And we at Fidelity feel that way, too."

Is now a good time to buy bonds?

Gray: "It's an okay time as long as you have a long-term time horizon. I'm not going to say bonds are going to be the best-performing asset over the next six months.

"But over the long haul, they will do well."

Loudon: "Bonds will do okay in 1988. You'll at least earn the coupon rate—8 to 10 percent—and probably do a little better than that."

Is the bear market in bonds over?

Gray: "It's hard to say. The market has changed dramatically. But it could change again. There are a lot of factors that influence interest rates, and no one really has a good handle on predicting what's going to happen to them."

Most economists are forecasting slow growth in 1988. Some are even predicting a recession. What does slow growth mean for interest rates?

(Note: See Chapter 1 for more on interest rates.)

Gray: "Low growth frequently leads to lower interest rates. Here's the reason. The government and the Federal Reserve usually introduce policies to stimulate the economy in order to get it back on its feet. And those policies are usually beneficial to interest rates—at least in the short run."

Suckow: "Any slowdown we have is probably already reflected in the price of the bonds, or conversely, the yield differentials between Treasuries and corporates. Right now, the spread between Treasuries and Single A corporate bonds is 100 basis points."

Will interest rates decline further?

Duffield: "It depends on what the Federal Reserve does. It depends on what happens in fiscal policy on the trade deficit side."

Anderson: "I see interest rates coming down."

Thorne: "There's no question that the meltdown has brought the likelihood of lower levels of earnings in the system and lower levels of inflation. So I think you can assume that there's going to be lower interest rates than there might have been otherwise.

"Granted, yield levels on bonds may get a little higher. But in a year, I think they will be where they are now or lower. In ten years, they will probably be significantly lower.

"Over the long term, I think interest rates will decline. Inflation has been discredited as an alternative by our fiscal policymakers. And the trend is clearly starting toward reregulation of currencies and the capital markets.

"The solutions to the worldwide problems of capital structures—debt, and so forth—are the stuff of lower interest rates and currency stability."

What does the forecast for interest rates mean to investors in bonds?

Anderson: "If you see interest rates coming down, you want to own bonds, and you want to own long-maturity bonds. And I see interest rates coming down."

Wyss: "With interest rates coming down in the short term, the best investment is going to be bonds. Even now, the real interest rate on bonds, real bond yield, is extremely high. Inflation is running about 4.5 percent, and Treasury bonds are yielding 9.0 percent even after the recent drop. That's a pretty good rate of return by historical standards.

What factors will influence the bond market in 1988?

Gray: "A better question is, what will affect interest rates and therefore the bond market? The answer: the rate of inflation, what's happening with the trade and budget deficits, the value of the dollar, the election, the strength of the economy, and the unemployment rate."

Thorne: "The vast majority of companies in this country are running scared. And they're trying to control costs. And that's all to the good.

"If any of the factors change—if you see unexpected problems that lead to inflation or disturb the dollar—expect interest rates to bounce up to 12 or 13 percent.

"But if such an event happens, it will happen and self-correct very quickly. Our system just can't afford that added burden of inflation without slowing down materially. And if it slows down materially, interest rates will drop some."

Suckow: "One factor that influences the bond market is the degree to which we have economic growth. Another is how the Federal Reserve responds to that growth—or the lack of growth. As we've seen, interest rates are driven cyclically by what goes on in the economy.

"Whether the crash slowed consumer spending, which, in turn, affects future economic growth, is still up in the air. I would argue that any slowing will be minor and short-lived, and we will be back on a path of reasonable economic growth.

"The bottom line? I think that this year—1988—is a good opportunity for people to assess and reassess their investment strategies and consider fixed-income instruments as an alternative to what they've been doing until now."

What types of bonds should perform best in 1988?

Suckow: "Corporate bonds, not Treasuries, will probably be the better performers in 1988—that is, if we don't have a serious economic contraction. If we do get an improved economy sometime in 1988, the spread in interest rates between Treasuries and corporate bonds will narrow.

"If, however, we head into a serious economic contraction in 1988, then Treasuries will do better than corporate bonds.

"But keep in mind that one year is not the time horizon people should be investing for. Investors, particularly in the fixed-income area, should look long-term, because the reinvestment of the coupon is such an incredibly important part of their total return."

Before we go into types of bonds and bond funds, let's review some bond basics. What's the difference between having a long time frame and a short time frame for bond investing?

Gray: "For starters, people should have a long outlook for all their investments. No one—not even the professionals—can call the tops and bottoms of markets.

"And people who jump in and out usually jump in and out at the wrong time. Had they taken a longer-term view, they probably would have done better.

"Of course, you can't always afford to have a long-term view.

But, as a general rule, timing the market isn't a good idea. Most people aren't very good at it.

"Summing up, bonds are good long-term investments.

"The returns over a long period of time are very good. They're slightly less than the returns for stocks over time. But bonds are also less risky.

"You're not going to double your money in six months by buying a bond. Bonds don't have the volatility of stocks. They don't go from a price of $2 to $20 in a few months.

"And you rarely, if ever, get a period where bond funds drop 30 percent in two weeks. Stocks can do that. But bonds aren't a get-rich-quick type of investment."

How do investors earn money from their bonds?

Gray: "You have to look at your total return, which has three components. First is the interest income that you receive. Second is the price change—either positive or negative—in the value of the security. Third is money you earn by reinvesting dividend income.

"With the rally in the bond market, most of the return was generated from price appreciation as the value of the securities increased dramatically.

"What people may not realize—but should—is that a significant part of your return over the long haul is affected by the interest income that you receive, plus the reinvestment of that interest over a long period of time. With stocks, the dividend is a relatively small part of the return. Most of the return is due to price appreciation.

"But bonds are called fixed-income securities, because they have a semiannual interest payment. And that's a significant part of your return."

Bond prices move inversely with interest rates. When rates go up, bond prices go down. When rates go down, bond prices go up. What's the reason?

Thorne: "Say you buy a bond at 9 percent, and interest rates drop to 8 percent. The bond price has to go up, because the yield of a bond is a function of price as well as the coupon rate—

9 percent in this case—and the coupon rate stays constant.

"Here's how it works.

"Your bond is yielding 9 percent and it's due in one year. Interest rates fall to 8 percent. The person selling the bond says, 'I want to get 8 percent for my bond.'

"So, you're going to pay that person $100 plus 1 point. If it's two years, you'll pay $100 plus 2 points. And if it's 30 years, you'll pay $100 plus 30 points."

I've decided to allocate a portion of my assets to bonds. What factors should I consider when it comes to choosing a particular bond or bond fund?

Gray: "The two main considerations are quality and maturity. So you want to consider credit risk, which involves quality, and market risk, which involves maturity.

"Let's talk about credit risk first.

"The highest quality in the taxable sector—credit-wise—are U.S. Treasury bonds, followed by government-agency securities.

"Next comes investment-grade corporate bonds rated from Triple A to Triple B, all the way down to junk ratings. Anything less than Triple B is subinvestment grade, or junk.

"Now let's turn to market risk. Market risk is a function of maturity. The longer the maturity, the greater the risk.

"That's because securities with longer maturities are more sensitive to changes in interest rates. Securities with shorter maturities are less sensitive to changes in rates. So, securities with shorter maturities are more conservative investments.

"You have to determine the level of quality risk you're willing to tolerate, as well as the level of market risk.

"Say, for example, you want very high quality with little credit risk and little market risk. You'd buy a U.S. Treasury security with a short maturity. If you want market risk but no credit risk, you'd buy a U.S. Treasury security with a long maturity."

Gordon: "See if the interest payments that are required to service the debt are covered two, three, or four times, depending on the nature of the company.

"Then select the bond with the highest yield.

"Remember, you don't have to be the senior debt holder. You could hold subordinated debentures if the coverage is adequate for everyone."

Are short-term bonds a good investment now?

Duffield: "I think short-term bond funds are a good deal for the short-term investor. In these funds, you get high yield and only moderate capital volatility.

"There are short-term bond funds—two to three years—on both the taxable and the tax-free side. They offer premium yields. Yields on the taxable side are in the 7- to 8-percent range and, on the tax-free side, about 6 percent."

Whether you invest in short-term bonds or bond funds really depends on your investment goals and objectives, right?

Thorne: "That's right.

"If you're 80 years old, and you think you may need to spend some of your principal to pay a hospital bill, you're better off buying a short-term bond than a long-term one."

What's the downside to buying short-term bonds?

Thorne: "The people who bought short-term bonds in earlier periods of uncertainty—when yields were high—had to reinvest the proceeds when the bonds matured. Then they were faced with the problem of reinvesting at 6 or 7 percent, and they didn't feel very good about that.

"So what's the worse risk? Is it worse to have a bond go up or down in value? Or is it worse to find out in four or five years that you may have to reinvest at 5 percent?

"As I said, the bottom line is you have to know your objectives. If you're my 86-year-old mother and don't want your income to go down, you should be all in 30-year bonds.

"On the other hand, if you have $200,000 that you're going to put down on a house in three years, you'd better go for lower volatility."

Now, let's turn to long-term bonds. What are the advantages of investing in long-term bonds?

Thorne: "If you buy long-term bonds now you'll lock in a good yield and will probably see your investment appreciate. But don't look at your investment every day. You don't price your house or your car every day. Don't look at your long-term bonds every day."

You buy long-term bonds for income, right?

Thorne: "Not exactly. You don't buy for income if you think the price is going to go down. That's a pretty tough way to feel good. You buy for income because you either think the price will remain stable or you're going to make some money.

"Otherwise, you stay away from bonds. And I say prices are going to be at least stable, and chances are, going to go up over the next three to five years."

Say I'm an investor, and I've allocated a portion of my portfolio to bonds. Where should I invest this money?

Gray: "It depends on your risk tolerance, your investment objectives, and your time horizon for your investments.

"Your first task is to identify your investment objectives over a period of time. Your second job is to determine how much credit risk and market risk you're willing to accept. Then you make your decision accordingly. Remember, each person is unique.

"Someone who has a high tolerance for risk and is investing long-term should be willing to invest in intermediate or even lower-quality bonds. These bonds have good returns over long periods—better than higher-grade investments. So if your time horizon is 20 years, a diversified portfolio of these lower-quality bonds probably makes sense.

"If you're very conservative and have little tolerance for risk, you should invest in higher-quality securities with shorter maturities, because these bonds are less volatile."

Thorne: "My advice is you probably should own more long-term bonds than short-term ones at least for the next year or two. Here's why.

"The critical threshold for judging bonds attractive is the real rate of return—the interest rate minus the rate of inflation.

"In the 200-year history of capital markets in this country, we never have had, for as extended a period of time, as much real return in the bond market as we have now.

"We have inflation running at 4 to 5 percent. Long-term bonds are yielding 9 percent, and the five-year bond is at 8.5 percent. So you're getting a real rate of return on your money the likes of which you've just never seen before.

"The reasons?

"First, the market reflects the volatility and the tremendous beating that bondholders took up until the early 1980s. When the horse gets to the part of the trail where the snake was last time, he's going to shy even though there's no snake there. So the market is very sensitive.

"Second, to the extent we're financing the budget deficit and have to rely on foreigners for capital, debt has to stay very cheap.

"And maybe it will stay very cheap for awhile. But the U.S. Treasury is prime-quality credit and is likely to remain prime-quality credit—at least in our lifetime.

"So you'll get a long-term stream of high-quality income, giving you 3 or 4 percent more rate of return than inflation and probably make some money, too.

"There are those who will tell you there is a real danger that inflation is going to stick its ugly head up again. But I think inflation has been substantially discredited as a tolerable alternative. The population is growing older and more conservative, and severe inflation would be a real threat to any politician.

"If you agree that inflation isn't likely to get much worse, you can make a pretty good case that these real rates of return on bonds are quite significant."

Kincaid: "Short-maturity bond funds are probably okay for the next 12 months. But, since I'm personally a conservative investor, I'd be less keen on long-term bond funds.

"Now is the hardest time that people have ever had in making investment decisions. So I would opt for shorter maturities, unless you're a very knowledgeable investor."

Loudon: "It depends on the investor.

"If you're looking for an appreciation play, if you think interest rates are going much lower, zero coupon bonds give you the most leverage.

"But if you're buying bonds for stability and income, it really hasn't paid off in the last few years to go out much beyond five, six, seven years' maturity. That's why I think medium-term bonds are the best place to put your money for reasonable stability and current income.

"With the inflation rate coming down—let's say 4 percent over the next year versus the 5 percent plus we would have projected before the crash—and five-year Treasuries going at 8 or 8.5 percent, you have a pretty good cushion over inflation.

"If you're buying a five-year maturity, you start to get the draw of the maturity pretty quickly. So the downside risk is limited."

Let's look more closely now at the types of bonds and bond funds available, beginning with Treasuries.

Busboom: "Treasuries are still attractive. The yields exceed the rate of inflation. But I wouldn't necessarily have all my money in them.

"The problem? You can buy a 30-day or 90-day Treasury. When that time period elapses, you have to reinvest, and you're vulnerable to reinvesting at lower interest rates. In a longer-maturity bond you lock in a yield for a longer period of time.

"But there's a tradeoff. Yields may go higher instead of lower. And then your longer-term bond goes down in price.

"My advice would be to have a mix. I wouldn't have all my money in short-term bonds. But I wouldn't have all my money in long-term bonds, either."

Now, Ginnie Maes and Ginnie Mae bond funds.

Duffield: "Ginnie Maes and Ginnie Mae funds offer pretty good yield premiums to people who are prepared for some short-term price volatility. If you have a medium-term outlook, you can get a very good yield on a Ginnie Mae fund right now."

Thorne: "Ginnie Maes are complicated. And the market for them is not as liquid as it is for Treasuries. The little guy gets reamed with the spread between bid and ask prices and broker's commissions. So the best way to buy these and other mortgage-related securities—particularly for the smaller investor—is through a good mutual fund.

"But you have to be careful. Some funds, in order to overstate their income, buy a high coupon (rate) at a premium. For example, the manager buys a 12.5-percent coupon at $108, say. Then, as people pay off their mortgages, you get your money back.

"But you get your money back at $100, not at $108. You lose eight points every time the loans are amortized. That means, of course, that the 12.5 percent is illusory, because if you keep getting paid off at $100 instead of $108, your effective yield is probably around 8.75 percent."

How do you avoid that kind of situation?

Thorne: "Read the prospectus. Make sure that the vast majority of the coupon rates in the portfolio are close to current rates. For instance, if current rates for mortgages are 10.5 percent, check that most of the issues in the portfolio are around 10, 10.5, or 11 percent.

"Ginnie Maes will fluctuate with the market. In any case, a mortgage is a lousy instrument, because it changes its characteristics. When you buy a bond you're looking for steady income and the fact that you're going to get paid at a certain time.

"But a mortgage doesn't work that way. When interest rates go up, the mortgage goes down in price. When interest rates go down, people pay off their mortgages faster or refinance. So you keep your mortgage-related security for a much shorter period of time than you thought.

"When interest rates go up, people pay off much slower so your cash flow goes down. And that's not really the way you want it. If you buy from a reputable fund, the fund manager will move the portfolio around to protect you against all these things.

"Ginnie Mae funds do make sense for people looking for current income who do not want to worry about quality. You'll have volatility, because the share prices will go up and down with interest rates. But that's interest rate risk, not quality risk.

"There's no risk your bonds aren't going to pay."

Let's move on to corporate bonds. What's the outlook for these bonds?

Duffield: "Corporate bond funds offer high yields at the moment—they're very attractive on a long-term basis. They offer a substantial premium over current and prospective inflation. But you're still subject to the risk of rising interest rates in the future.

"They're a good investment for someone with a medium-term time horizon, but not for someone who's unwilling to take any principal risk."

Gray: "It's not a good idea for individuals to buy corporate bonds on their own unless they can have a diversified portfolio. You should own several issues, and you should have each issue be just a small portion of your portfolio.

"People should stick to high quality, but I don't think anyone should go out and buy ten-year General Motors bonds and have those be the only position in his or her portfolio. They're good quality, but you're not meeting one of the basic principals of investing—to diversify."

Thorne: "High-grade corporates certainly have a place in a portfolio. But I would add two notes of caution or, rather, words of advice.

"First, make sure the bonds are reasonably high-grade and look like they're going to stay that way. To help you there, you need a source of credit analysis, which is widely available throughout the brokerage fraternity and from publications such as Moody's and Standard & Poor's. Stick with a good solid Single A or Double A, depending on the industry.

"A Single A utility, for example, without much nuclear exposure, means a lot more to me than a Single A commodity chemical company.

"Second, make sure you buy at a good price: The bonds ought to yield at least 1.5 percent to 1.75 percent more than Treasuries.

"You also have to watch out for callability—the right of the company to buy back your bond before it matures. If you're going to take the risk of owning a long-term bond and you think it's a good idea, you don't want it taken away from you. Or buy a bond at a deep discount so you don't care if it's called.

"Also, remember that it can get awfully expensive to trade bonds. That's another reason for getting paid a fair amount of additional income."

Do you like any specific corporates?

Thorne: "There are some interesting rails, though they're somewhat lower quality. I think Missouri Pacific 4.25-percent bonds due in 2005 are quite attractive and, for a shorter-term deep discount bond, Atchinson Topeka General 4-percent bonds due in 1995.

"The railroad's somewhat controversial because it's just undoing a merger with Southern Pacific, but the Atch has always been a gold-plated railroad."

How do convertible bonds look today?

Thorne: "You can make some money—particularly when the stock market is sick—in depressed convertibles. And you can get convertibles for companies such as Xerox or American Hospital Supply with a rating of from B to Double A. You should buy them at a discount.

"Xerox with a 6-percent coupon due in 1995 is probably worth about 85 as a straight bond without the conversion feature.

"You either get 6 percent a year for seven years and get 100 for a bond that cost you 91, or maybe the stock will do something. The point is, to pay a cheap enough price for it when the market isn't particularly enthusiastic about convertibles.

"If you've a good stomach, Wang 9-percent convertible debentures due in 2009, which are now trading at about 85 are attractive. Wang is probably going to make it. Wang got hit pretty hard, but it's going to survive. It's yielding over 10 percent, and you might make some money.

"American Medical is also attractive. Owning American Medical with a reasonably high coupon at a discount is going to be competitive over a period of time if you're patient.

"Convertible bond funds will be less volatile than the stock market. They'll yield more, and they're probably okay. But you have to look at the prospectus and see what quality the fund's buying.

"If there are names you recognize, and they sound like they are a good representation of corporate America, that's one thing. If they're all Consolidated Moose Pasture convertibles or something similar, that's something else again."

Markese: "Convertibles are a reasonable way to go, because you have the potential to participate in a market upswing. You're getting a consistent interest payment, and they're less volatile than the common stock held directly. But it's hard to get diversification in this area unless you go through a fund."

Johnstone: "Convertible bonds are less attractive now than they were prior to the crash. They do have their place. And, in fact, I am buying several now.

"But, in general, here's what happens. Convertibles hold up well in a decline. But after they've already declined, they're less likely to have a bounce. In other words, they have a lesser amount of upside potential to rally back to where they were.

"It's better to get into convertibles in the later stages of a bull market. Then, if the bull market keeps going, the convertibles will go up just like stocks.

"After you've already crashed, the convertible has already taken on the characteristics of a bond. And, usually at the bottom of a crash, the convertible sells at an excessive premium to conversion.

"So you'll not get much of a bounce in the convertible, because the common stock has to go up so far before the convertible feature kicks in.

"That's why convertibles are not generally what you want to buy at this stage of the market. You want to be in more aggressive common stocks—unless you're very bearish. If you're very bearish, you probably shouldn't be in the market anyway—convertibles or otherwise."

What's the outlook for junk bonds?

Busboom: "In the current environment, I'd look less favorably on lower-quality, higher-credit-risk corporate bonds.

"While we aren't forecasting a recession, we do think growth will be quite slow in the first half of 1988. So we could have a business environment where it's difficult for companies with a lot of leverage to generate the kind of cash flow they need to service their debt.

"And in a slow-growth economy with some risk of recession, you're better off not getting too involved in these highly leveraged companies."

Duffield: "Junk bond funds have been rattled by the stock market. They offer very high yields at the moment compared to what they've traditionally offered relative to U.S. Treasury bonds or federal agency bonds. The key here, though, is the economic outlook.

"The market is very concerned about whether there will be an economic recession and how junk bonds would do in those circumstances.

"Personally, I think the yields available on high-yield bonds amply reward investors for the increased risk. But you'd want to be in a fund that is well diversified, with many issuers and with a bit of the better-quality issues."

Loudon: "I would not buy junk bonds. I would stick with quality, because I'm sure the panic is going to have some impact we can't foresee.

"I would stay away from low-quality bonds that are likely to have fundamental problems on top of market problems. The spreads have widened, but we don't think they've widened out to the point where it makes sense to accept the extra risk."

Gordon: "The problem with junk bonds isn't so much the risk of default. It's a problem of liquidity. You go to sell and the old joke is, to whom? Either you're forced to hold or you're forced to absorb a greater-than-anticipated loss."

Thorne: "If times are a little bit tough—which they may be—the market becomes quite credit conscious and prices of lower-quality bonds tend to go down. Having said that, though, there's an awful lot of good junk bonds around.

"Some smaller issues of some of the cable companies are good. These guys have the wires out and they have the customers, and people aren't going to disconnect their televisions. The companies are highly leveraged, but the cash flows are there.

"I also like Bethlehem Steel 4.5-percent debentures due in 1990, which are trading for about 82. You can make an 18-point profit at the end of three years. And the company's not going to go bankrupt, unless times get a lot tougher than people think they will.

"Also, some of the utility bonds that have had trouble with state regulation and nuclear problems—for example, Louisiana Power & Light—are good bets, though I'm not talking about utilities, such as Seabrook in New Hampshire, that are in big trouble.

"I would, however, stay away from junk bond funds.

"If Mom and Pop are sitting down in the sunshine, and their fund's net asset value drops from $13 per share to, say, $9.5 per share, it's going to bother them—even if the fund keeps paying them income."

People are starting to talk a lot these days about foreign bonds. How do they look for investors?

Eveillard: "Six months ago we were between 15 and 18 percent in foreign equities. And we haven't changed our allocation that much.

"But we own more foreign currency bonds than we do foreign equities. We are 25 to 30 percent in bonds, mostly short- and medium-term foreign currency bonds. One of the better opportunities in this area are five- to ten-year bonds in deutsche marks or Swiss francs.

"I started diversifying outside of the dollar and buying foreign-currency bonds in the spring of 1984. I was almost one full year too early. Then the decline in the dollar was so tremendous over the following two years, that I have enormous profits in those bonds."

Are there any funds you'd recommend?

Donoghue: "I like the T. Rowe Price International Bond Fund, which is paying a return better than the money funds—maybe 8 or 9 percent.

"The fund benefits from interest rates falling internationally and from the dollar decline. So you have a double whammy working there. It's also an intermediate-term bond fund, with the maturity of most of the issues from three to five years.

"And many of the securities are either government bonds or bonds that are implicitly backed by governments. So we're not talking that much risk."

Let's turn to zero coupon bonds. Why should people invest in zeros?

Gray: "The advantage of owning a zero coupon bond is that you have no reinvestment risk. Whatever yield you buy it at, that is the yield you will receive over the life of the bond as long as you hold it to maturity.

"It's a good way to put away X dollars today and in 20 years, you'll have four to eight times that amount, depending on the yield to maturity at which you buy. This is due to the reinvestment of interest earned each year but not paid out.

"As long as it's high quality, for example a U.S. Treasury zero, you can be comfortable that you're going to get the full face amount when the bond matures. So it's a good investment.

"But people should realize that zeros are the most volatile of bonds, especially long-term zeros. So if you have to sell your zero before maturity, you could end up selling it for a different amount than you might otherwise expect. Because zeros don't have annual interest payments, like other bonds, the price moves more dramatically with changes in interest rates."

Should investors buy zeros now?

Thorne: "Zeros are cheap now. But my advice is to stay with Treasury zeros. If you're in a zero that is issued by a company and something happens to that company, your claim is subordinate to a regular bond. Besides, Treasuries have better marketability.

"But be aware that there's a big spread between the bid and ask prices. Brokers charge horrendous commissions relative to the total value of the principal.

"If I were buying a zero directly, I'd try to get a banker to do it for me, and I would get a friend in the business to quote the wholesale market. Call up First Boston and ask, 'Where would a million zeros due in 1995—a million strips—trade?' Then see what you're paying.

"And I would also insist on a commission report, which means that the broker has to tell you what he or she paid for them and what you're paying in commission."

What about U.S. Savings bonds?

Thorne: "They're just another type of zero coupon bond. Just be sure you check the yield before you buy."

Lastly, municipal bonds.

Gray: "Municipals, like corporates, have credit risk and market risk. Of course, the advantage of municipals is that income you earn is exempt from federal taxes. It's exempt from most state taxes, too, if it's issued in the state where you pay taxes—for example, you buy a municipal bond issued by the state of New York and you're a resident of New York.

"Changes in the tax law of 1986 made municipals one of the most attractive tax shelters around, because the law virtually eliminated all other tax shelters. So from that point of view, municipal bonds are more attractive than they used to be. However, the same tax laws also reduced marginal tax brackets, making municipals less attractive."

Thorne: "Municipals are cheap. The yield of municipals—relative to Treasuries—is high. You're subject to the same short-term volatility concerns that you are with any part of the market. But I suspect we're going to be paying more taxes than less over the years.

"So this is a good time to buy munis.

"Municipals, though, are a highly fractionated, inefficient, negotiated market with high spreads between bids and asked.

"If you have a fair amount of money, hire somebody who uses professional traders to manage your portfolio. Or buy a reputable bond fund. But always read the prospectus, and always make sure the quality of the bonds is what you expect."

Markese: "I'd stay with municipals in the short- to intermediate-term area—no more than seven years. Rates may go up again. So you're looking for income with stability of principal."

Kincaid: "Municipals are awfully interesting right now, because the whole municipal supply this past year has been so small due to the changes under tax reform.

"The market certainly has an increased volatility.

"But for people who are in high tax brackets, tax-free funds or the individual municipal bonds are really an important part of their portfolio."

Gordon: "I'm bullish. Municipal bonds of good quality offer attractive yields on an after-tax basis."

4

QUICK FIX?

The Outlook for Equities

If we knew today what the stock market was going to do tomorrow, well, we'd all be rich by the day after. But who knows?

There is always someone who can tell you how you *should* have invested, what stock you *should* have bought, or what stock you *should* have sold.

But that advice was valuable yesterday, not today. What you're looking for is information that will help you make investment decisions now and in the months ahead. Do the experts know where the postcrash market is heading? Of course they don't.

But what they do know—about the external forces that are likely to affect the market and about the way industries and companies are likely to respond—can help you make the wisest and best informed investment decisions possible.

In this chapter, top investment strategists, stock market analysts, and mutual fund portfolio managers take a look at the factors that will affect the market in 1988.

Here are the experts featured in this chapter:

- Charles Allmon, chairman and president of Growth

Stock Outlook Trust, a closed-end fund, and editor and publisher of the *Growth Stock Outlook*, an investment newsletter in Bethesda, Maryland.

- Peter Anderson, senior vice president for IDS Financial Services in Minneapolis, Minnesota. IDS is a subsidiary of American Express.
- Gavin Dobson, portfolio manager for the Kemper International Fund, a mutual fund operated by Kemper Financial Services in Chicago.
- Jeremy G. Duffield, a senior vice president of The Vanguard Group of Investment Companies in Valley Forge, Pennsylvania.
- Steven G. Einhorn, partner and co-chairman of the investment policy committee at Goldman, Sachs & Co., an investment bank in New York City.
- Jean-Marie Eveillard, portfolio manager for the Sogen International Fund, a mutual fund based in New York City.
- Monte Gordon, director of research for the Dreyfus Corporation in New York City and a regular participant on public television's "Wall Street Week."
- Mark Hulbert, editor of The Hulbert Financial Digest, a Washington, D.C.-based publication that tracks the performance of investment newsletters.
- C. Bruce Johnstone, managing director of Boston-based Fidelity Investments and portfolio manager of Fidelity's Equity Income Fund. He also serves as senior vice president and income-growth group leader for Fidelity Management and Research, a subsidiary of Fidelity Investments.
- Douglas M. Loudon, managing director for Scudder, Stevens & Clark, which has its headquarters in New York City.
- John D. Markese, vice president and research director for the American Association of Individual Investors in Chicago.
- Andrew H. Massie, managing director for Scudder, Stevens & Clark. He serves as portfolio manager for

Scudder's Capital Growth Fund and AARP Capital Growth Fund.
- David F. Saks, a stock market analyst for L. F. Rothschild & Co., an investment bank with headquarters in New York City.
- Arch Spencer, portfolio manager for the IDS New Dimensions Fund, a product of IDS Financial Services in Minneapolis.

Here's what our experts had to say.

Did you see the crash coming?

Einhorn: "I foresaw lowered stock prices. But I didn't have any sense that it would come with quite the ferocity and swiftness that it did."

Allmon: "We were looking for the market to go off the cliff. On August 23, two days before the market hit its top, I told a reporter for the *New York Times* that I thought the Dow was going down 35 to 50 percent. But, even before then, our fund was almost 80 percent in cash."

What did you tell your clients?

Einhorn: "We told our clients in early September to move to their maximum cash levels and their minimum equity levels, whatever those happened to be.

"We have our own model portfolios for institutional investors. And in those institutional portfolios the maximum cash reserve for us tends to run around 40 percent.

"We were suggesting to people that whatever your maximum in cash happens to be, go to it. And whatever your minimum happens to be in equities, go to that, because we felt the markets were vulnerable."

Why did you think the markets were vulnerable?

Einhorn: "We felt they were vulnerable for a couple of reasons. First, stock prices were unusually high relative to earnings, dividends, book value, and interest rates. We had achieved record levels of valuation on those various benchmarks.

"Second, we were concerned in the summer months by the slowdown in money growth and the acceleration in GNP growth in the United States.

"The relationship of money and GNP is important to the markets, because, when money growth is a lot higher than GNP growth, there is excess liquidity, which can flow into financial assets. And when there is money growth that is only equal to or less than GNP growth, there is no excess liquidity that can flow into stocks.

"And that imbalance has tended to be troublesome. In fact, in the summer months, money growth just equalled GNP, and we were concerned.

"Third, we were concerned by what appeared to be a worldwide tightening of monetary policy and rising interest rates.

"Finally, we were bothered by the very slow progress being made on our trade deficit. It appeared that a lower dollar exchange rate by itself was not having the effect on the trade balance that most people felt it would.

"So we combined all those things, and it said to me that the market was vulnerable.

"What bothered me, in particular, was that we had such an unusual level of valuation at a time when money was slowing down in growth and interest rates were rising.

"Historically, that's been a fairly poisonous combination, so we expected shares to move lower. And we went to our maximum cash position."

Where do you think the Dow is heading now?

Anderson: "Over the next two years, we will not only return to the 2700 plus level, we'll be over 3000. That means a rate of return for stockholders of 50 percent over the next several years. That's not peanuts, plus you've got dividends."

Massie: "It's going to take a long time to reverse the negative psychology that the crash created. But I don't think we're going to a level much lower than the one we reached on Black Monday. I don't think there's a huge amount of upside in the next six to nine months.

"Then the Dow will work its way higher. It may even get to

2200 or 2300 sometime in the first part of 1988. But then it will move back down. It's going to be in a trading range of, say, 1700 on the low side to 2250 or so on the high side, for quite some time, maybe even a year.

"Then what direction it takes is a function of how the economy reacts to the problems before us and what actions, if any, are taken on the federal budget and trade deficits."

Allmon: "We still think the market has a long way to go on the down side. The decline is not over by any means. We've yet to see the big selling climax.

"What we saw on Black Monday was a selling panic induced by programmed trading. But the big washout won't come until all these open-end mutual funds start to unload.

"Remember, there are 15 to 20 million people sitting out there who have losses in all those open-end mutual funds, and those people are going to start selling.

"People forget that the last 200-point drop in the Dow in 1974 was caused primarily by the forced liquidation of open-end mutual funds.

"This selling spree is going to be a bigger washout than we saw on October 19. It won't come in one day, though. It will come over a period of six months to a year.

"Before it's over, though, we're going to see the Dow somewhere between 1100 and 1400. And I expect to see that low in 1988 but no later than the first half of 1989.

"We've had a great big financial joy ride, and the party is over. But I suspect the hangover may be longer than the party."

Markese: "First, let me sum up what everyone else is saying. Everyone else is looking at 1929 when we saw the market decline, rise again, then really fall off. And a lot of people are looking for a cookie-cutter pattern of that period.

"They're looking for a rise in the next six months to the 2100 or 2200 range, then a real decline again, maybe below the previous low of 1738.

"But I don't believe in cookie-cutter history.

"The economy still seems awfully strong. Inflation is very, very low—not a threat at all. The lower dollar will start boosting sales of U.S. goods to other countries. The trade deficit may decline a bit, and it looks like someone's finally going to do something about the budget deficit.

"So I would say we'll trade within a range of 1800 to 2100 for maybe six months to a year. I wouldn't forecast a tremendous updraft in the market, nor a crash. I just think it will move sideways or maybe even deteriorate some to the 1800 level."

Loudon: "The Dow did run up to an extreme level. For instance, those who were in portfolio insurance had higher stock positions than they would have otherwise. To the extent that was a factor, it probably pushed the Dow to an artificially high level.

"So, with the thought that every day is brand new, we think it's reasonable to expect that, during 1988, the Dow will climb 10 percent to 15 percent higher.

"Undoubtedly, there will be some resistance in a technical sense if the market gets up to 2300 or 2400. People will start selling, because they fear the market is getting too high, especially now with a lower-growth economy.

"But we think the Dow has seen its low.

"The panic low during the day on October 19 was around 1650. We see a low somewhere around 1650 to 1700. We expect the market to trade in the broad range from 1700 to 2100 for a while."

Gordon: "There will be volatility without question.

"Moves of 50 or 60 points in the market are nothing these days. Many people speak of a trading range, that is, a low of 1738 and a high of 2100 to 2200.

"But this is a market that is trying to find itself—to find a trend that's acceptable. It's not a trading range in the sense that you're moving back and forth, because nothing is motivating you. You're moving because of the market's uncertainties and its inability to make clear-cut judgments about where it's going.

"I would say, though, that 1738 would be the low, and the high would be somewhere around 2100. Once things fall more into place—for example, you get a budget-deficit program and the dollar begins to stabilize—the market will move higher.

"I do think the bottom has been made. The world, in a sense, did end on October 19. It did change. And there is a new world emerging. But its parameters are unclear."

Are stocks undervalued now?

Massie: "I'd say they're probably fairly valued. They're not terribly undervalued, and they're not terribly overvalued.

"Of course, these things become clearer in retrospect. But let me say that the market was too high when long rates—that is, rates on long-term Treasury bonds—got up to 10 percent and price/earnings (P/E) ratios were in the range of 17 to 18.

"Long-term rates have come down to a little under 9 percent. And P/E ratios have come down a lot more than, say, the 10-percent decline in interest rates.

"P/Es, in my judgment, are fair right now."

Eveillard: "Obviously, stocks are a better value when the Dow is at 1900 than when it is at 2700. But even at 1900, it's still almost two-and-one-half times book value.

"So the values aren't tremendous.

"Don't get me wrong. There are some outstanding values—mostly over-the-counter—but the overall market is not an outstanding value.

"I don't mind stepping up to the plate and being fully invested when I think I'm buying stuff cheap, but the stuff is not cheap yet."

Markese: "We're at a point where stocks are relatively at a bargain. And I don't mean just looking at them from what their price was previously, but looking at basics like P/E ratios, dividend yield, and price-to-book-value ratios."

Loudon: "Stocks aren't cheap, but they're fairly priced. We see a compression of valuations. You don't pay as much for quality these days, and that's a plus. And you don't pay a premium for growth stocks either, and that's another plus."

Duffield: "Over the long term, common stocks look reasonably valued. They're not outrageously good buys. But people may want to look at small-company growth stocks and funds. The small-company area has been beaten down since 1983."

Gordon: "From an historical perspective—and I think that is the perspective you should take—stocks are quite reasonably valued."

Is now the time to buy stocks?

Gordon: "There's no urgency to go into the market now. Someone going in should recognize there is a possibility that prices will go lower. In that case, they should take advantage of the drop and increase their investment."

Duffield: "Investors might get back into the market if they saw a stronger economy and strong prospective earnings growth.

"And the third-quarter numbers for corporate profits were very strong relative to 1986. A lot of the bulls were depending on these strong profits.

"If, over the next year or two, corporate profits continue to kick up in the wake of a strong economy, the stock market is going to go higher."

Allmon: "We're in a primary bear market, whether anybody wants to admit it or not. Everybody's been running around scooping up so-called bargains, but they're going to find to their horror—maybe this year—that these bargains are going to be even bigger bargains.

"We're managing about $425 million, and we're holding about 80 percent cash right across the board. We're not about to change that stance."

What advice would you give stock market investors in the wake of the crash?

Spencer: "Buy quality companies, well-known companies. These can be growth companies, but I would stay away from speculative situations."

Eveillard: "Be patient. Be conservative. Buy value. Don't look at the stock tables every day."

Massie: "If investors have any cash reserves, they ought to be carefully looking at some small- and medium-sized companies.

"I wouldn't rush right in right now, because there is an awful lot of uncertainty. But I would begin to do my homework.

"If I found something that's really an outstanding value, I'd start to buy it now. And I'd continue that buying between now and, say, the second quarter of 1988.

"I would concentrate on small- and medium-sized growth companies that are less sensitive to the economy, because there are uncertainties about the economy.

"If investors follow this approach, they'll end up putting together a portfolio of well-priced, attractive companies that will make a lot of money for them."

Markese: "Investors should realize that we always have the potential for a dramatic decline. And they have to put a portfolio together that they're comfortable with.

"They have to adjust their portfolio now to a point where they can maintain their long-term financial plan and still endure a 30-percent decline, say.

"The easiest approach is not necessarily to sell off securities but to build up cash positions. But I would recommend that most people trade any extremely risky investments for cash.

"As far as looking for new stocks to buy, I'd look for common stocks that had large price declines not based upon any fundamental change, but just the market crash.

"In other words, I'd look for stocks that have a record of earnings increases, that have maintained a dividend if they had one, and that are selling at reasonable price-to-book values. Reasonable would be 1.5 price-to-book value or less—that is, price-per-share to net-worth-per-share, or what the net value of the firm is worth per share.

"I'm also a contrarian.

"So, if I was going to buy, I'd say buy in the industries that have been beaten down the most, the ones no one wants.

"Now's the time, for example, to buy Salomon Brothers or some of the strong regional brokerage houses—A. G. Edwards, and so forth. They've all been hit and the industry looks terrible. It takes guts, though, to buy these stocks, because these companies are reporting their losses now."

Loudon: "Start with the small growth companies and take a look at the large growth companies. Also, try to find growth companies with foreign exposure.

"The dollar has declined so dramatically that, without any

doubt, you're going to see at last the benefits of transatlantic earnings. Manufacturing companies, for example, are now fully competitive again, which they haven't been for a long time.

"And the drug stocks have some of everything. A lot of them have foreign exposure. They have consistent growth. And in many cases they have reasonable valuations as well.

"Bristol-Myers is a very cheap stock. So's Sterling. Merck probably has the best combination of everything, but you pay extra for it. But some of the hospital supply companies—Baxter and Johnson & Johnson—look reasonably priced.

"Smaller companies have higher risks just because they have bigger competitors. The best way to play those companies is through the small-growth-company mutual funds.

"We'd advise investors to avoid the more exposed consumer stocks, because the first thing people do when they get a little concerned about the economy is stop buying cars and washing machines and that sort of thing. So we would stay away from consumer durables.

"You also have to be very selective in the technology area—that is, hardware—because of foreign competition. The software area should continue to grow. There's always the question of high prices for these stocks, but the United States has a big advantage here."

All investors, especially those who are still in the market, want to know what to do now. So let's run through a few scenarios. Say you're an investor who has lost a lot of money in the market. Should you cash out now? Or should you sit tight?

Loudon: "It depends on what stocks you now hold. If the stocks are lower-quality issues, you probably ought to at least upgrade to higher-quality ones. From a tax standpoint, I'd say take your losses in 1987. Don't wait until 1988.

"But I wouldn't tell you to take the losses and get out completely. I'd tell you to take the losses and see if you can upgrade your portfolio without paying too much more, which we think is possible today."

What about investors who are in, say, an aggressive growth

mutual fund and saw their share value drop more than 30 percent. Should those people stay in or get out?

Markese: "I'm going to assume that if they put their money in the fund in the first place, they had a long-term investment horizon of at least five years. If not, they shouldn't have been in the fund in the first place. They should have realized that the fund is very volatile.

"But to pull out now would compound this mistake.

"Five years from now, I'm sure they'll be much better off than today. If they face a hefty tax bill, they may want to take their loss and reinvest in a similar fund."

Where should people who want conservative investments look?

Markese: "All our research shows—no surprise—that if you're looking for conservative investments, go for a higher dividend yield.

"And look for a higher dividend yield not caused by distress but by the ability and willingness of the firm to pay dividends.

"Those stocks dropped the least in the last market."

What's a good yield?

Markese: "If you're looking at utilities, a good yield is probably about 8 percent. But you don't want to go too high or you're in a speculative situation.

"Anything above 9 percent is probably speculative in the utility area. A reasonable yield for a nonutility stock is around 4 percent."

INCOME-ORIENTED STOCKS

What type of investor should be interested in high-yielding, or income-oriented, stocks?

Johnstone: "All investors should be interested in these stocks except those at the extreme ends of the risk spectrum. People who want to hit home runs and are aggressive, risk-taking stock investors should not be invested in high-yield stocks. You don't hit home runs with high-yield stocks.

"Likewise, people who have very low-risk profiles and cannot afford capital depreciation at all should not be in stocks—period.

"All other investors seem appropriate for these stocks. Here's why. You get downside protection. You get the comfort of income, and you get low volatility. Plus, you get investments in senior securities—that is, bonds and convertible securities—all of which tends to dampen the downside risk.

"But you do not lose that much as far as upside potential is concerned. A well-managed portfolio can perform almost as well as the market, particularly if you add in the total return that can be generated by income alone.

"So, with the combination of above-average income, the compounding of that income, and judicious stock selection, you can have almost as much upside potential as you would with most portfolios.

"But people should realize that we have just had a crash of record proportions, that the risk of recession and reduced economic activity is higher certainly than it was before the crash, and there are risks of negative earning surprises. So investors might want to reduce the percentage of their portfolios that's in stocks."

Do you look for some minimum level of dividend when selecting stocks?

Johnstone: "The cutoff or trigger point for me is the market yield. That doesn't mean I never buy stocks that yield less than the market, but that's my starting point.

"When the market was its highest, the yield was down as low as 2.5 percent, a very, very low yield for the average yielding company in the S&P 500, which I take as a proxy for the market. The yield now is about 3.5 percent, because the stocks have come down so far and dividends haven't been cut."

If people wanted to invest now in the income-oriented area, what would you suggest?

Johnstone: "Before the crash, we were advocating getting very, very defensive, because bonds had gone down while stocks had gone up.

"Now, bonds have rallied strongly and stocks have crashed, so the two have come back together. That means you have many more choices in the income-oriented equity area.

"So you could have a fairly broad exposure of stocks in the universe of companies that I follow—that is, all the securities with above-average yields. Within this high-yielding universe, a combination of defensive and offensive stocks is a good diversification strategy."

Could you define offensive and defensive?

Johnstone: "Primarily, I'm talking about volatility. Defensive stocks are likely to move more slowly on both the upside and the downside.

"If the world falls apart economically, offensive stocks are going to be more vulnerable. If it doesn't, these stocks will bounce up more sharply."

What industries and investments would you put in the defensive category?

Johnstone: "Banks, telephone utilities, electric utilities, insurance stocks, convertible securities, such as convertible preferred stocks, and convertible debentures, straight debentures—that is, nonconvertible bonds and preferreds—and perhaps a slightly larger percentage of cash reserves than you otherwise might normally have."

Defensive Investing

What's your favorite defensive equity category?

Johnstone: "I feel very strongly about bank stocks, particularly regional banks. This area of the market is extremely undervalued. These securities were undervalued before the crash, and now they're exceedingly undervalued.

"They're selling at less than half the market multiple, half the market price-to-book value, and have well-above-average dividend yields.

"And there's a tremendous amount of bad news that is already public information and, therefore, probably already reflected in the price of the stocks. So I'm perhaps more bullish on regional banks within the defensive category than other areas."

What should investors look for when evaluating regional banks?

Johnstone: "You'd want to see how well capitalized the bank is—that is, how much equity it has versus assets. This measure gives an indication of the financial stability of the bank.

"A company that has more than 5 percent of its assets in the form of equity is a well-capitalized bank. With a company under 4 percent, you have to be skeptical.

"The quality of the loan portfolio is also critical. Does it have less than 2 percent of its loans outstanding that are nonperforming?

"If more than 3 percent of a bank's loans are nonperforming, you start to get a little more nervous. Does it have a very large exposure to LDC loans—that is, lesser-developed-country loans, such as Brazil, Argentina, Mexico. If it does, you have to be even more skeptical.

"Also, very important are loans that the bank has made that are not yet nonperforming but may become nonperforming. For example, you get a little uncomfortable with banks that have made a lot of leveraged buyout loans and banks that are heavily into Texas real estate."

What regions of the country do you like as far as banks go?

Johnstone: "Michigan is a dramatically improved region, and New Jersey regional banks are also very much improved. Pennsylvania, upper New York state, and Florida are quite attractive. New England has been very attractive. It may be getting slightly less so, but it's still quite attractive.

"California isn't quite as good. Texas is horrendous. Avoid Texas. The Middle Atlantic is pretty good. It's still too early for the Southwest and Colorado—they still have major problems with real estate, energy, agriculture, and so forth."

What other defensive areas appeal to you?

Johnstone: "Telecommunications is a very interesting long-term story. First, the telephone utility companies are growth companies. The unit growth rate of telephone traffic in this country is well above average.

"The only reason these stocks do not traditionally sell at the premiums or the multiples of growth companies is that they're regulated.

"So if you could somehow diminish the negative of regulation, you've really got something going for you. You have a consistent-growth business, cheap stocks, and above-average yields.

"That's why we're so excited to see that there really are developments to reduce regulation. For example, with AT&T, there's talk about changing from regulating return on equity to regulating price. This change would allow the telephone company to grow its earnings if it can do it without raising prices above a certain rate vis-à-vis inflation.

"The regional Bell operating companies are the same story. They are beginning to get positive regulation from the states within which they operate. Nynex, for example, has struck a deal with the state of New York public utilities commission to get a joint sharing of the profits that come out of cost savings.

"The problem is, it's going to take a few years for the regulatory authorities to allow deregulation. So we have an emerging growth company story within a very high-yielding defensive group. It's a very nice combination. Over the long run you're going to make money with the stocks, yet all the while you have your downside protected.

"And the stocks are attractively priced right now.

"Telecommunication stocks and banks are long-term investments. You could hold these for years and make a lot of money."

Turning to electric utilities, would you avoid those that are involved in nuclear plant construction?

Johnstone: "It depends on the security. Probably 80 percent of the utilities in the country have something to do with a nuclear-generating plant, and there are lots and lots of utilities that have handled that situation very well.

"The only ones I would stay away from are those with a significant unlicensed nuclear power plant that is very controversial regarding how much of the plant was or was not prudently built. You want to know how much of the costs could be considered imprudent and, therefore, disallowed. In that case, the company could earn a rate of return only on the lesser amount that the state commission felt was prudent.

"And there are a number of these utilities. The yields are very very high, but the risks are equally high. Either the dividend may be in jeopardy or you simply won't have any growth at all.

"For example, Public Service of New Hampshire, Gulf State Utilities, or Long Island Lighting all have serious financial exposure to unlicensed nuclear facilities."

What industries would you consider in your offensive categories?

Johnstone: "The offensive categories are more cyclical. The stocks in these industries had terrific upward price moves prior to the crash and have corrected dramatically. Many of them are beneficiaries of a weaker dollar. So even if there is less strong economic activity ahead, these companies may do well.

"Here's why. These companies have regained market share from companies in foreign countries that were taking their markets when the dollar was stronger.

"Specifically, stocks in this category include chemicals, metals and mining, paper and forest products, office and electrical equipment, machinery, and even railroads. The United States was exporting very little steel or grain when the dollar was strong. But now the railroads are back in business.

"Exports of coal are likely to pick up, grain traffic is picking up, lumber product shipping is picking up, domestic mills are shipping more steel because we're backing off foreign imports of steel, and the transportation of chemicals has grown—again, because we're backing off the importation of chemicals and fertilizer and so forth.

"So, in general, these industries are weaker-dollar beneficiaries because we're backing out imports, we're increasing exports, and the price of our products is no longer under the same downward pressure, because competition from imports is so much less than it was two-and-one-half years ago.

"A lot of these stocks really got creamed in the crash. They had been going up before the crash. But because the crash made everybody so fearful of a recession, and these are cyclical companies, the stocks got the hell beat out of them. So they became available at prices that, in my opinion, discounted a recession.

Which industries in this category appeal to you the most?

Johnstone: "I like virtually all chemicals. There aren't many steel companies that still pay a dividend, so I would say the dividend-paying steel companies. And US Steel may be the only one.

"Again, not too many metals companies pay dividends. But when there are convertible preferreds—for example, many of the copper companies, such as Phelps Dodge, Noranda, and Inspiration Resources offer convertibles—there's quite a bit in the way of copper that you can buy.

"The aluminum stocks got whacked in the crash. And so virtually all the aluminum stocks with dividends are attractive.

"And practically all dividend-paying railroads—CSX, Conrail, Burlington Northern, and Norfolk & Southern, for instance—became attractive."

Are there any other categories you like?

Johnstone: "There are very few stocks in the office and electrical equipment category—IBM and Unisys are notable exceptions—where there is a yield.

"Machinery is very tough for me to play even though, intellectually, it's attractive. But there's almost no yield in the entire group, which is really a shame.

"Gas is also a very interesting area."

What appeals to you about gas stocks?

Johnstone: "First, I don't know whether you call gas stocks offensive or defensive. They really have a lot of the characteristics of both: Yields are high and the companies do have utility subsidiaries. But the stocks performed very poorly, because the price of gas has been surprisingly weak. The price of oil rose sharply from $6 to $20 a barrel over the last 12 to 14 months, but the price of gas has actually gone down. It's really bizarre. And it's really gas-on-gas competition.

"That is, there's just too much gas around. It's not that there's too much in the way of competitive fuels, because oil certainly doesn't compete with gas at these prices.

"But we think the gas glut is temporary for a number of reasons. The consumption of gas is rapidly eating into reserves, the amount of gas being drilled for is not adequate to satisfy more than a year or two of incremental needs, and long-lived reserves are disappearing rapidly.

"Moreover, less Mexican gas is available because the country is burning it internally to boost Mexican oil exports. The situation is similar in Canada, although some Canadian gas does come across the border.

"So we see a shortage of supply developing with a continuing increase in demand and an extremely low-priced commodity that is temporarily out of sync with the price of oil. Those are the reasons we're very interested in gas. And the stocks are incredibly cheap in terms of price-to-cash-flow, price-to-dividend, and price-to-book values."

Do you see any other interesting areas currently?

Johnstone: "Autos are interesting, because the stocks of all three major U.S. auto companies are selling at extremely low multiples of earnings. Ford's selling between three and four times earnings and Chrysler at about three times earnings.

"General Motors has a higher multiple, because the yield is so much higher. And the General Motors dividend has cushioned the stock on the downside. So GM has declined to a six- to eight-times multiple area.

"All three have cut costs, General Motors significantly. Most importantly, the weak dollar has made foreign imports of automobiles no longer anywhere near as competitive and as attractive as they used to be. So automobiles are, again, a great dollar play.

"The auto companies are obviously at greater risk in a recession, however. So they may not be quite as attractive as some of the other groups.

"For precisely the reasons you might want to own a U.S. auto manufacturer, you might not want to own a foreign auto manufacturer. That is, the dollar has been weak against most of the countries—even Korea—that export automobiles.

"The foreign autos are exposed to both the risk of recession and the risk of lower exports, since the cheap U.S. dollar has backed out imports of foreign automobiles. And the U.S. market is the largest market in the world for automobiles.

"The other group I would buy is aerospace stocks. You're getting an extraordinary amount of technology in companies that you're buying at extremely depressed prices.

"You're also getting very attractive dividend yields, because the whole world knows the defense budget is being cut and airlines are having some financial difficulties. So everybody knows that business is going to be okay, but not great, in the next several years.

"But the stock market has discounted those problems too heavily. So these stocks are attractive on a relative valuation basis."

What areas would you avoid?

Johnstone: "I would be very leery of Japanese stocks in general. From a valuation point of view, those stocks are selling at very high multiples, very high price-to-book value, and very high price-to-dividend values—relative to history, relative to U.S. stocks, relative to the risk of earnings growth going nowhere or possibly even turning negative, and, finally, relative to the amount of debt and real-estate speculation that is underneath the Japanese market.

"Foreign stocks really aren't my area, but I think that whole scene is scary.

"I'd also put in the avoid category, stocks in countries where you've had strong currency movements vis-à-vis the U.S. dollar.

"These countries are at great risk for dramatically slowing economic activity, because their exports are in trouble and foreigners are going to begin taking market share. Besides, valuations—particularly in the case of Japan—are starting at such high levels.

"Domestically, I probably would avoid gold stocks.

"But there really aren't a whole lot of domestic categories that I would avoid at this time. You could almost say that, as of the afternoon closing prices of October 19, the market fell so sharply that the entire recession was already discounted. So that's why I'm not so sure you want to be terribly negative. Cautious, yes, but not negative.

Did your funds in the equity-income group perform in the crash as you would have expected?

Johnstone: "Yes, they did. We outperformed the market because we do have above-average yields and lower volatility.

"We have downside protection of income with senior securities in the portfolios, specifically convertibles and straight bonds. Before the crash, the stock market was up 35 percent and my fund was up 20 percent. The day after the crash, I was ahead of the market."

Have you made any shifts in your investment philosophy or tactics as a result of the crash?

Johnstone: "Yes. Tactically, I took advantage of the decline to get into some of the more offensive stocks. Before the decline, all the cyclical, lower-yielding, dollar-beneficiary stocks were in the stratosphere. They were really inappropriate in terms of yield for my investment style.

"After the crash it was suddenly like being in a candy store. There were stocks available to me that I hadn't seen in a couple of years in terms of price, yields, and price/earnings ratios. It was unbelievable. So I definitely got more aggressive after the crash than I had been before it."

Did you increase the percentage of cash in your portfolio?

Johnstone: "Our cash went up a little—in the neighborhood of 4.5 percent—just to make it convenient in case shareholder redemptions picked up significantly, which they didn't. The crash was almost a nonevent for my fund in terms of redemptions."

What about the other funds in Fidelity's equity-income group?

Johnstone: "We all got a little more aggressive after the crash. Before the crash, we were more nervous than we had been in a long long time, because valuations were at all-time historical highs.

"So we had been more cautious and defensive. We had all sold chemicals, paper, and office equipment stocks, and technology in general. I had sold even some consumer stocks, such as Kodak and Ford, where we had made huge amounts of money.

"I had moved, for example, out of Kodak and into the Baby Bells. That's the kind of thing we all did before the crash. And it really paid off.

"After the crash, all of a sudden, a stock such as Arco Chemical, which had gotten as high as $38 or $40 a share, moved down all the way to $17. An unbelievable backoff. And Arco is an excellent company with very good growth potential.

"So, in general, we reversed to some extent what we had been doing before the crash because no longer were the values so ridiculous. The defensive stocks we'd bought before the crash held up. They provided us with the powder we used to go back into the more aggressive stocks after the crash.

"Of course, economic activity now has a much greater likelihood of slowing in the next 12 months than was the case just two months ago. So if we got into some of these very aggressive cyclical stocks on the lows and we make 20 percent, we might be more likely to take some profits without waiting until we get back to 2700.

"That is, if the market goes up again, we may begin to reduce the high beta nature of our fund."

So where do you see the Dow heading?

Johnstone: "I'm no guru. I don't know if we're going to 2600 or 1500. But given that the market is a great discounter of future activity, my guess is that a recession has already been largely discounted.

"And the rally off the lows—the low got as low as 1620 on an intraday basis on October 19—to more than 2000 a few weeks later, maybe partially discounted a recovery already from the recession.

"So I wouldn't be surprised to see a trading range in the stock market that anticipates slower economic activity—but a lot of that has already been anticipated.

"Whereas earnings estimates for 1988 by all the analysts were just up 15 to 18 percent, now we're starting to see earnings estimates come down to plus 5 or 10 percent. And, in some cases, we're seeing negative numbers.

"The market is beginning to adjust to the new economic reality. And I would not be at all surprised to see a trading range, maybe up 200, down 200."

What do you do then?

Johnstone: "If that's the case, when the market's up 200, you scale back and get out of some of your more volatile stocks and into some of the defensive areas that haven't participated in that 200-point advance and vice versa.

"If we go back down 400 from that point—that is, 200 below the middle point—you sell some of the defensive stocks that did the job for you in the decline and get into some of the more aggressive stocks. So I may well take advantage of the volatility of some sort of a center point by buying the securities that are depressed and selling ones that are expensive.

"But all the while, and this is very important, I keep in mind the company's fundamental characteristics which we observe.

"We visit thousands and thousands of companies every year. We're always on top of the economic situation of a company, an industry, and the economy as a whole. So, again, when I say we'll be buying and selling securities, it's always within that context.

"Obviously, when you visit a company and things are better than you expect, you're less likely to trade out of its stock on a rally. Likewise you're likely to buy more on less of a backoff than you otherwise might."

So would you advise individuals to change their investing strategy?

Johnstone: "I might have slightly more cash reserves than I would have had a year or two ago, or even three or four years ago. There is a slightly greater chance of an economic accident than there was. And there is a slightly greater chance of a market crisis. But I want to emphasize that I always put these things in the context of odds.

"Anytime you're investing in the marketplace you simply have to assess the odds. And I think the odds have shifted a little.

"That's what's really changed over the last two to three years. The crash around the world changed the economic odds, the speculative bubble in real estate and the stock market that built up in Japan have changed the market odds.

"Since the odds are a little different, you might want to be slightly more cautious, slightly less aggressive vis-à-vis your cash exposure to stocks and to real estate for that matter.

"But this is a shift. It shouldn't be a batten-down-the-hatches, climb-into-your-bunker mentality."

GROWTH STOCKS

Let's talk about growth stocks a moment. What's the outlook for these stocks?

Duffield: "I think the outlook is uncertain. They're probably not outrageously overvalued at the moment. But it's unclear whether there is great near-term potential.

"It's probably a decent time to accumulate good growth company stocks and good well-managed growth-stock mutual funds on a long-term basis—say five to ten years. But I wouldn't accumulate them as a way to make a near-term killing."

Loudon: "The small-growth companies were left behind in this market. They peaked in mid-1983, and they've declined ever since. Right now, they're very cheap.

"Our own Scudder Development Fund, which invests in small-growth companies, had a valuation premium of about 125 percent in mid-1983. Today, it's selling at a 10- to 15-percent discount to the market. These are the same companies growing at the same rate.

"The reason they've been left behind is that foreign investors typically don't buy secondary stocks. They buy the stocks of big companies they know and understand, the ones that are easy to follow and have been a factor in the market.

"The second reason growth stocks have underperformed the market is index funds, which, by their very nature, buy more big stocks than the small ones."

Massie: "If you look at the S&P 500, you'll see that the 100 biggest companies constitute about two-thirds of the index. And the biggest companies have been far outperforming the medium-sized and small companies for four years now.

"That trend also held true in October.

"The 100 largest companies in the index outperformed the index by 2.5 percent. The 100 smallest companies, as a group, underperformed the index by over 12 percent.

"Everyone now is talking about buying blue-chip stocks, buying safety, buying big companies, buying liquid stocks.

"That strategy may be correct in a very short-term sense, but, in any long-term sense, it's going to be proven absolutely the wrong road to have taken.

"The values in this market are in the small and medium-sized companies, in the growth stocks, which have not been the performers in recent years."

As you said, these stocks have lagged the bull market throughout. And everyone keeps saying that their turn will come. But it hasn't happened yet.

Massie: "It's true. It hasn't happened yet. And it's continued to be bad for these stocks throughout October. There's nothing to say that the turn has come.

"I am saying, however, that this situation is going to change and—just given the length of time over which this trend has gone on—it's closer to turning now than it was a year ago.

"For example, Kidder Peabody does a monthly study of the 50 growth stocks that have the highest price/earnings ratios. It compares those ratios to the market. In the 16 years they've done that study, growth stocks have never been as cheap as they are today.

"Now, that tells you something. Maybe it gets still cheaper next month. But the study tells me that we're in a low area. Some of these are premier companies, and they're as cheap as they've ever been in recent history relative to the broad market.

"My simple point is that people ought to be prospecting for small- and medium-sized companies, because there's going to be a change. If you take a two- or three-year time frame, you're going to make a lot more money in the issues of these small- and medium-sized companies."

How would you tell investors to go about looking for these stocks?

Massie: "*Value Line* is a good source of information. It covers around 1,800 companies. When you look at small- and medium-sized companies, search out those that aren't overly sensitive to the economy, since we're in a period of economic uncertainty."

Do you have any growth stocks to recommend?

Allmon: "There's always something worth buying out there. And let me tell you we have big positions, in seven figures, in all the stocks I mention. We put our money where our mouth is.

"People should look carefully at a real estate investment trust (REIT) called **New Plan Realty**. (Symbol: NPR. Exchange: NYSE.)

"We think it's the best REIT in the country, because it has about $100 million in cash, and the principals have never sold any stock in the company since they founded it back in 1972. It's just a well-managed company.

"We also like **Hughes Supply**. (Symbol: HUG. Exchange: NYSE.) It distributes building materials in the state of Florida. It's selling at a low P/E multiple. It's well below book value, and it's been growing steadily. We expect it to keep on growing for some years.

"**Angelica** is another stock we like. (Symbol: AGL. Exchange: NYSE.) They're in the laundry business. They pick up uniforms, launder them for you, and deliver. There's nothing very glamorous about it. They just keep on making money.

"And we like **Harleysville Group**. (Symbol: HGIC. Exchange:

NASDAQ.) It's also selling under book value. They're in the property and casualty insurance business. It's a spinoff from the old Harleysville Mutual Insurance Company, which still owns about 70 percent of the company. The company's a good solid operator.

"These are bear market plays. These stocks are not going to fall out of bed. They're going to be around five years from now, that's for sure.

"These are not Micky Mouse companies by any means."

Massie: "You can just go down the list. It really is unbelievable. Take **Student Loan Marketing**, which has grown in the past three years at 29 percent per year without a down quarter. (Symbol: SLM. Exchange: NYSE.) It ought to grow at 20 percent a year for the next three years. It's trading at 14 times 1988 estimated earnings at just a small premium to the market.

"You can come up with gobs of these issues in the growth-stock arena where the pricing is just as cheap as it's been relative to the market in decades."

(Note: See the next chapter for other stock picks.)

Any other industries and companies that stand out?

Massie: "We've been buying stocks in the pollution-control area. These stocks aren't very sensitive to an economic downturn.

"We don't know for sure whether the economy is going to go into recession. We're not banking on one, but I think it's quite clear the economy will be slowing.

"Pollution-control stocks are down by at least one-third—in a lot of cases, even more. In these companies, growth is going to continue at a pace of 20 to 30 percent, no matter what the economy does. Yet, the stocks are down to prices that are compellingly attractive.

"We've liked and added to a company called **USPCI**. (Symbol: UPC. Exchange: NYSE.) **Union Pacific** just made a tender offer for all the stock at $25.

"The biggest industry group in our portfolio—about 8 or 9 percent—is cable television stocks. Most people aren't going to disconnect their cable if things get tight.

"These companies are interesting for a number of reasons, but one of them is the fact that the whole industry was deregulated at the end of 1986. So for the first time in their history, they're able to price their product the way they think it should be priced.

"They're not misusing that right, because they do have monopoly control in most markets. But, for the first time, they're moving their prices up at a clip of 5 to 6 percent.

"These stocks came down in line with the market during the decline. But now we think they're even a more compelling value than they were before."

Are there any other industries you consider recession proof?

Massie: "Investors should look at some of the really bashed-up stocks, where a given industry has been destroyed or tarnished by the poor earnings reports of a few. Specifically, we like some of the specialty retail stocks. **Charming Shoppes** is an example. (Symbol: CHRS. Exchange: NASDAQ.)

"These stocks have been destroyed, cut in half. Yet, when the dust settles, I think these stocks will reassert themselves as leaders."

MUTUAL FUNDS

Now, let's turn to mutual funds. What kind of funds are best for investors these days?

Gordon: "I would look for growth-and-income funds, sometimes referred to as all-weather funds. They don't perform as well on the upside, but they don't go down as much either."

Duffield: "High-yielding funds are a conservative way to participate in the stock market with current income to buffer the market volatility."

What about balanced funds?

Duffield: "Balanced funds also offer a conservative way to stay in the stock market and invest in both the stock and bond markets. They offer very generous yields at the moment, in the neighborhood of six percent. They should fit the needs of most people who are willing to take a moderate amount of risk."

What's your view of sector funds now?

Duffield: "It varies by sector. Investors have to be very careful. They really should invest only with the people who are most aware of what's going on in various sectors, people who really want to watch the market on a day-to-day basis.

"I don't think there are very many of those folks."

Gordon: "Sector funds defeat the purpose of a mutual fund. The mutual fund says to the investor, you select your objective and let the manager make the selections. A mutual fund is broadly diversified. Professional management selects the sectors and areas of emphasis.

"With sector funds, on the other hand, you're asking the investor to make the selection. If I think chemicals are attractive, say, I buy a chemical sector fund.

"But if something happens to that sector, I'm in terrible trouble. Look at the performance of the Fidelity sector funds in the crash."

FOREIGN STOCKS

On to another topic: international or foreign stocks. How did these issues fare in the crash?

Dobson: "They collapsed like everything else. There was nowhere to hide."

Which market did best?

Dobson: "In dollar terms, the market that fell least was the Japanese. It was odd, considering everybody was expecting the crash to start there, then work its way around the world. Japan was down only 5.8 percent for the entire month of October."

How did the equities of other countries perform?

Dobson: "Of major markets, Japan was followed by Copenhagen, down 6.5 percent. Then there is a big gap, and you get to Sweden down 17 percent, Frankfurt down 17.9 percent, Paris down 20.1 percent, London down 22.2 percent, Switzerland down 20.4 percent, and Toronto down 23.2.

"Amsterdam fell 23.8. Singapore was down 39.9 percent, Taiwan was down 41.2 percent, and Hong Kong fell 42.8 percent. And Australia tumbled 44.5 percent. So, basically, everything fell off a cliff pretty much in tandem."

How did your fund and some of the other international funds hold up?

Dobson: "Our fund was down 22 percent, kind of middle of the road. We did a brief checkup with our competitors, and we're right in the middle. Of international funds, the best was down 17 percent and the worst fell about 38 percent."

Up to the crash, had your fund been doing as well for 1987 as international funds did in 1986?

Dobson: "We were trucking along very nicely. In 1986, our fund was up 34 percent. In 1987 BC (that is, before the crash) we were up 34 percent. We were well on track to making more than 40 percent, if things hadn't happened the way they did."

Are foreign stocks overvalued?

Eveillard: "I don't think foreign stocks provide outstanding value. Some provide better value than others. I think the worst is the Japanese market. That's one thing that worries me. Some day, the Japanese market is the other shoe that will drop.

"So the Japanese market provides less value, say, than the German or the Swiss market or, for that matter, the U.S. market."

Are foreign stocks still attractive?

Dobson: "Foreign stocks now represent 64.5 percent of the total world market. So the answer has to be, yes. If you're interested in equities at all, you have to look overseas. But as always you have to be highly selective."

Where are the bargains in foreign stocks?

Dobson: "I hate saying 'go international' without being able to substantiate it. So let me take you through our portfolio.

"As of November 24, 1987, **Canada** represented 5.8 percent of our fund. We have a very strong mineral flavor there. In spite of the crash, we like some of the mining and natural resource stocks—Noranda, for example, which is a very diversified company.

"We also like Seagrams, not necessarily because of its beverage alcohol division, although that's doing very well. But it owns a big percentage of Du Pont, which owns Conoco. So, by extension, it is a resource stock.

"A lot of the natural resources in Canada are waking up after a long period of slump in the early 1980s. Therefore, a company such as Canadian Pacific, which runs a railroad, is also interesting to us, because they're shipping these natural resources to the Pacific ports.

"After the crash, we've seen 1987 highs in copper prices. We've seen nickel firming. We've seen aluminium in a tight supply situation.

"And a lot of these stocks are quite a long way off their crash bottoms. For instance, Inco, the nickel stock, hit $13 a share and now it's up to nearly $18 U.S. dollars.

"The first thing that the world thought of on October 20, when it woke up with a big headache, was that the crash was potentially deflationary.

"People were thinking immediately of 1929 and the 1930s. And, therefore, they wanted to get out of anything that was remotely a proxy for inflation.

"That's why the mining stocks in Canada and Australia got absolutely blitzed. But a lot of minerals, mining stocks, and metal prices themselves have hit their 1987 highs since then. And that tells me that the real economy is still fairly robust.

"We have 1.3 percent in **Denmark**—just two stocks. The Danish market didn't fall very much during the crash.

"We have 2.1 percent in **France**. We're slightly ambivalent about France. There are a lot of world-class French companies, but there are significant political tensions there with a presidential election coming up in May 1988.

"Mitterand and his Socialist party are going to do their best to destabilize the economy, to discredit Mr. Chirac's right-wing party. So we expect political agitation coming up ahead—

strikes, for example, which will not be healthy for the stock market.

"We have only two stocks there. One is BSN, the food company. It owns Dannon yogurt, for example, in the United States. The other, at the opposite end of the vice scale, is Moet Hennessy—the champagne stock. If the polls started to go against Mitterand, we might take a heftier position in France.

"In **West Germany**, we have 6.2 percent. There are a lot of very good values in the German market. Take a company like Bayer, the drug company, on six times earnings and compare it to Merck, which is on 28 times earnings.

"But the Germans are not big equity owners themselves. They're conservative and tend to be bond and cash oriented. The German leadership is not doing much to stimulate the economy. So we're not dashing into Germany.

"**Netherlands**, where we have 2.3 percent, is linked to Germany. If Germany starts to take off we would also pile into the Netherlands. Our biggest holding there is Unilever.

"In **Norway**, 0.8 percent of our portfolio, we have just one stock—Norsk Hydro. This company represents about 30 percent of the Norwegian index. It's a major extractor of natural gas and North Sea oil, has metal smelting, and so forth.

"In **Switzerland**, we have 5 percent. On the one hand, we focus on companies, such as Nestle and Swiss Bank Corp., because those are the stocks that foreigners rush to in the flight to quality. Then we have some cyclical companies, such as Brown Boveri, the engineering concern, which is coming off the ground.

"On the whole, we quite like Switzerland, because it's a very tightly run economy. It has low inflation, virtually no unemployment, a strong currency, and a strong high-tech sector. Also people like owning Swiss francs in times of stress.

"We've really been adding to the **United Kingdom** part of our portfolio—we're up to 24 percent, the biggest position in six years. We have several reasons. One is tight economic management. The country is basically well run, with a balanced budget, tax rates and unemployment heading down, inflation and the trade balance under control.

"And here are some unlikely statistics: British manufacturing productivity is rising at twice the rate of the Japanese. The economy is expected to be the fastest growing in the Western world in 1987 and possibly into 1988.

"On the micro side, British companies, on the whole, are cash rich. They're profitable and much more competitive worldwide, because of the massive corporate restructuring in the early 1980s.

"We have two broad categories of stock in Britain: The first consists of big exporting companies with significant earnings in the United States—for example, companies such as British Aerospace, Jaguar, and the conglomerate BTR.

"We think these companies will do well, because sterling is now more than $1.80, and if the dollar rises in 1988, these companies' earnings in America translated back into sterling will be good.

"Another part of our British portfolio consists of companies that have above-average growth in their own right—for example, United Engineering Industries, which is a small conglomerate, and Dixon's Group, a retail company.

"Even if there is a downturn in world trade next year, Britain is fairly well-positioned. The next part of the British scene to do well should be the domestic economy, such as the Northeast or Liverpool. Those areas are so depressed that they can only go up. Labor costs are low, and the union problem is substantially under control.

"So we own companies, such as Storehouse, which is similar to Crate & Barrel in the United States, leisure stocks, such as Mecca Leisure, which runs cinemas and bingo and so forth, and United Newspapers.

"In **Hong Kong**, we're just over 2 percent. Our holdings there are all related to hotels and land and real estate.

"We're operating on the principle that the Hong Kong dollar has gotten so beaten down relative to the Japanese yen that the Japanese are pouring into Hong Kong. It's sort of a bargain basement for them. So we own Hong Kong Land and Paliburg, the hotel group.

"Essentially, though, we're blah on Hong Kong.

"We have 36.2 percent in **Japan**. Japan may be overvalued globally on a price/earnings basis, but the fact remains that it's now, by some measures, the largest stock market in the world in dollar terms. It's a huge, sophisticated, diverse economy.

"So there is always something to buy, always some sector that is depressed or due for a bounce, or some part of the economy that's experiencing above-average growth.

"We have three broad areas of stock in Japan. One consists of the obvious ones: the big diversified international blue chips, such as Hitachi, Honda, Mitsubishi, and Matsushita.

"When the yen rose, everybody wanted to get out of any stock in the export sector, because their earnings overseas would be hit.

"They were hit, but the stocks were hit far more than their earnings. We also like these companies, because a lot of them have quickly become global multinationals.

"Take NEC for example, which makes its laptop computers for the U.S. market in Georgia.

"Then there are all the car companies starting up in the States and in Europe: Nissan, for example, growing very rapidly in Britain, and Toyota in Kentucky.

"So these companies aren't really currency sensitive anymore. If sterling suddenly took a dive, they could switch production to Britain, or if the deutsche mark took a dive they could switch production to Germany.

"For example, a lot of the Japanese plants in the States are bigger than the domestic U.S. market needs. And you're going to see Toyotas exported from the United States back to Japan.

"Our second category in Japan is what I would term a secular play. The domestic sector is going to grow steadily for 5, 10, or even 20 years. So we like companies involved in restructuring the infrastructure, in building roads and buildings, in laying drains, in putting in sanitary ware—that is, toilets and baths.

"It's very low tech, but it's a very real area of growth in Japan. As the yen has risen, more and more Japanese are travelling overseas and seeing how well foreigners live, particularly the Europeans and the Americans. They say, 'We're twice as rich as these guys, why do we live half as well?'

"So there is a big long-term demand for these things. That's why we have a whole range of companies such as Nishimatsu Construction, Maeda Construction, and Tokyo Construction. We also have my favorite stock, Toto, the biggest manufacturer of toilets in the Far East.

"Our third category consists of depressed cyclicals, all in the machine-tool area. These are companies such as Mori Seiki, Sonoike, and Murata Manufacturing. They're all cheap, and they really have not participated in the Japanese boom of the past four years. We think their time is about to happen.

"**Australia** makes up 6.6 percent of our portfolio. We got so blitzed in our resource stocks there, we didn't even attempt to sell. But we still see value, even though our stocks got clobbered. We've doubled up on CRA, which is a big conglomerate mining company. In fact, in Australia we principally have mining stocks.

"**Singapore** makes up 3.2 percent. We see Singapore as one country—Singapore/Malaysia. The political situation is looking a bit ragged there.

"But if you exclude political tensions, the economic outlook isn't bad. It's very dependent on commodity prices, such as rubber, cocoa, and palm oils. Cocoa hasn't done much this year, but palm oil prices are up 45 percent. Rubber prices are rising. We have a couple of stocks there, such as Malayan Banking and Inchcape, which is a trading company."

Do you think the international scene is going to improve?

Dobson: "We have only 3.4 percent of our fund in cash. And that should tell you that we're not too worried about what the world has to offer. In the middle of October, we had up to 14 percent in cash. So, in our view, the emergency is over."

What's your view of the dollar in the next year?

Dobson: "Our company view is that the dollar is very oversold. And we think it could sell off more and become cheaper yet.

"But the event that the weaker dollar was designed to create—an improving U.S. trade balance—is very much in the pipeline. I see this happening all around America. For instance, every steel mill in Gary, Indiana is working flat out.

"We feel that the U.S. trade balance is going to improve in the first quarter of 1988, and this improvement will be suddenly recognized in the currency market. From its final oversold position, the dollar has a potential to rise 20 to 25 percent next year."

Would a rise in the dollar have a negative effect on international funds?

Dobson: "It depends on how they're structured. Since we're anticipating this development, we have a lot of dollar-sensitive stocks. West Germany's Bayer, for example, derives 25 percent of its revenues from the United States. If the dollar rises next year, Bayer and companies such as Hitachi, Toyota, Jaguar, and British Aerospace, will do well.

"If you're loaded up on Japanese utilities and domestic stocks around the world, your fund could get hit. But if you're loaded up on international trading stocks, such as our Japanese machine-tool stocks, the rising dollar will be very good."

What tips would you give investors who want to buy foreign stocks?

Dobson: "There are about five different ways Americans can invest overseas. One is to simply pick up the phone to their broker in Zurich and say, 'Buy me such and such in Switzerland.'

"The good news is that this way is probably the best way of doing it. The bad news is that you have to have about $1 million so you can take advantage of economies of scale. So this method is really restricted to the institutional markets.

"American investors can also buy an ADR (American Depository Receipt), which can be listed on the New York Stock Exchange, the Amex, or Over-the-Counter. There are currently over 600 ADRs, which gives you a pretty good spread of stocks around the world.

"They're denominated in U.S. dollars. And you can buy them through your stock broker in Chicago or Oshkosh or wherever.

They behave the same way as American stocks in the sense that you have a five-day settlement period and and you don't have to concern yourself with the currency.

"But the information flow on a lot of these companies tends to be limited, certainly for the retail investor. So you really have to know what you're doing.

"Also, you're paying a bit more for your ADR. A bank sets the ADR up and charges a fee for it. And because most retail brokers in the States are not dealing in a huge amount of ADRs, you usually have extra brokerage costs as well.

"There's another, more strategic, problem with ADRs. Usually foreign companies come to America to be listed for one reason. And that's not because they like American shareholders so much.

"They want to have access to American capital markets. They tend to be the more mature foreign companies—the Hanson Trusts, the Hitachis.

"The more interesting, fun, fast-growing little foreign company doesn't list itself over here. Still if you catch the companies that do list at the right moment, you can do very well.

"The third way you can go overseas is to buy global funds—big safe funds, such as Templeton, which has maybe 45 or 50 percent of its assets invested in the United States.

"The fourth way is to go to the opposite extreme and buy a single-market fund, such as the Korea fund, Mexico fund, India fund, Italy fund, France fund, and so forth.

"Most of the single-market funds are closed-end funds, though some of the regional funds, such as Merrill Lynch Pacific Basin, are open end.

"If you catch one of these funds right, you can do extremely well. For example, earlier this year the Mexico fund rose from $3 to $14 or so.

"I would be careful of the closed-end funds though.

"When they get launched, there is a great hoo ha saying we're now going to launch the Bangladesh fund. And you think, 'Why are they launching this fund now?' If you look carefully, you'll usually find that the Bangladesh stock fund has had a tremendous run up, and it's close to its all-time high.

"That's why I would advise anybody, 99 percent of the time, to wait until the aftermarket, and not to buy one of these closed-end single-market funds on the offering.

"The only exception to the rule was the Korea fund.

"All the other funds got launched and then got clobbered. If you're really enamored of a particular region and a fund comes out, my advice is to wait.

"The fifth category, where the Kemper International Fund fits, is the general international fund that invests everywhere in the world except for the United States.

"Some of these funds are load, some are no-load, some are big, some small, some are conservative, some more aggressive. We're all slightly different from each other."

How should an investor evaluate one of these funds, especially in the postcrash environment?

Dobson: "It's very important to establish that the fund is run by a team or manager with a lot of experience and depth.

"I'd also look at the fund's defensive qualities. Obviously, in a bull market, you want a high beta fund, such as Fidelity Overseas. In a bear market, you want a low beta fund, one which is more conservative, such as the Kemper International Fund.

"I don't think we are in an uninhibited bull market anymore. It's not dead, but the easy money has been made and lost. So I would certainly choose a manager who has good defensive capabilities."

How can you tell from the prospectus if a fund is defensive?

Dobson: "I'd look for a lot of stocks with low multiples—that is, the big blue chips, such as Bayer, Unilever, and Hitachi. The companies should also have high earnings visibility, a good income stream, a lot of new products, and good representation around the world in consumer staples, for instance.

"For example, Unilever owns Chesborough Ponds. In Japan, we own a company called Kao Soap, which is Japan's Procter & Gamble.

"And I'd check for a preponderance of small illiquid markets. I'd be leery of any fund that is loaded with companies in Italy,

Spain, Finland, Norway, Philippines, Korea, or Taiwan, for example. Big positions in big markets is a good indicator of a fund's conservativism."

What's your favorite foreign stock?

Saks: "Glaxo Holdings is rated as the number one, most attractive drug company in our drug industry investment scorecard, with high marks in every category.

"Glaxo gets the highest marks in profitability among all 14 companies in our universe and also superior scores in current prescription trends, past financial performance, future earnings momentum, patent strength, and research capabilities.

"Glaxo is the largest pharmaceutical company based in the United Kingdom. We view it as a world-class drug research organization and dynamic growth company.

"Six years ago, Glaxo ranked twenty-third among world drug firms, but is now positioned in about fifth place and should move into third place in the foreseeable future.

"Their most significant new drug success includes expanded uses of the world's most popular-selling ulcer drug, Zantac, for teating ulcers. Zantac continues to gain market share. Glaxo has leading market-share positions in antibiotics and respiratory compounds.

"The stock is underowned by U.S. institutions."

INVESTMENT NEWSLETTERS

In the last few years, investment newsletters have boomed. Now, more than a million investors rely on these publications for advice. Which performed best in the crash?

Hulbert: "First, let me point out that one can too easily take this question out of perspective. When the market was surging upwards and some newsletters were doing really well in a given month, we were telling people that one month does not a track record make. The same thing should be said on the way down.

"I recognize that people focus more on the downside than they do on the upside. After all, it's much harder to give up capital than to forego profit. The real question is: Are the rules changed now? Is it a whole new ball game? I don't see that it is."

Why do you think the game hasn't really changed all that much?

Hulbert: "Immediately after a crash, a lot of indicators may not have that much validity, if you look at them short-term.

"But the results of my work and other academic researchers suggest that short-term strategies, on the whole, have not been all that effective anyway. Individual investors, particularly, should invest more for the long term.

"When an individual investor tries to play a shorter-term game the odds are really stacked against him or her. And that fact hasn't necessarily changed. October was undeniably bad, but don't forget it came after an unprecedented bull market.

"Some newsletters were out of the market before the crash. But some of these were out sufficiently far in advance that they gave up a large amount of profit. So some people who were fully invested and took a bath in October were still further ahead than those who got out."

How many newsletters do you track?

Hulbert: "We track about 210 portfolios in about 105 newsletters. Many of the letters run model stock or mutual-fund portfolios. If they don't, we construct a portfolio for them under preannounced rules and procedures."

So which portfolios weathered the crash best and why?

Hulbert: "Standouts would include Martin Zweig of the Zweig Forecast. He actually made money on the day of the crash by having a hedge in his portfolio—a one-percent position of OEX puts that more than made up for the losses of the stocks.

"OEX is the S&P 100 index, the most widely traded index. Zweig bought in at around $2 and sold out at $130. He was ahead for the year going into the crash, and, after October, he was even further ahead.

"Other newsletters that got out in time include Richard Russell's *Dow Theory Letters*, *Telephone Switch Newsletter*, the *Investech Market Letter*, and *The Professional Tape Reader*.

"All of these are ahead for the year.

"Newsletters that issued sell signals after the close on October 15 include *Harry Browne's Special Reports*, *Mutual Fund*

Strategist's "investor's" timing model, and *Sector Funds Newsletter.*"

"Several other services gave sell signals immediately before October 15, giving subscribers more advance notice. These include *The Dowse Market Letter*, *The Dines Letter*, and *Systems & Forecasts.*

"In addition, the *Lynn Elgert Report*, the *Elliott Wave Theorist*, and *Stockmarket Cycles* all issued sell signals in early October—although the last two had reentry advice that they aborted just in time.

"Overall, the five that did best in the month of October were: *Puetz Investment Report* (aggressive portfolio up 2705.9 percent, conservative portfolio up 565.4 percent), *Garside Forecast* (up 25.9 percent), *The Option Advisor* (average gain, 16 percent), *Switch Fund Timing*, (up 14 percent), *Princeton Portfolios* (formerly *High Technology Investments*, average gain 5.11).

"The five that scored best for 1987 to this point are: *Puetz Investment Report* (average gain 526.6 percent), *The Option Advisor* (average gain 64.6 percent), the *California Technology Stock Letter* (up 63.1), *Tony Henfrey's Gold Letter* (up 60.1 percent), and *Your Window Into the Future* (average gain 58.9 percent).

"People should keep in mind, however, that a letter such as the *Puetz Investment Report* follows an incredibly risky strategy. Its aggressive portfolio was all in puts. So it's way out ahead. But whether that lead is sustainable is another question.

"One last point: The average newsletter was growing more cautious—that is, was recommending slightly less exposure to equities—before the crash."

Which did the worst?

Hulbert: "The *Prudent Speculator* is one. It was the number-one ranking newsletter going into the crash. And it was fully margined. So it was a very risky way of playing the market and, indeed, paid the price for it.

"Nevertheless, it was sufficiently far ahead that even after taking a nearly 60-percent loss, it's still ahead of the market for the last seven years.

"Again, that's the point I want to stress about perspective. It's sufficiently far ahead that it's still beating the market, and there aren't that many newsletters that can say that."

What tactics seem to have worked best?

Hulbert: "As it turns out, there are good and bad technicians and there are good and bad fundamental analysts, so it's not as though one can come up with an answer to that question for all time.

"The people who take a more buy-and-hold approach end up making more on the upside, because they don't prematurely get out of the market. They also suffer more on the downside.

"It's an open question over the long term which technique will turn out to be better. The question doesn't admit of an easy resolution."

So how should investors judge these newsletters?

Hulbert: "I would look at a track record and see if there's a solid basis for expecting a gain to continue. If a newsletter has done well but has been a stopped clock—it has simply ridden the wave—ask how it's going to do if the market turns against it.

"If somebody has caught some major swings and hasn't always been a stopped clock, one's more willing to expect that their experience was due to something other than luck.

"Just because a newsletter had a big loss in October doesn't mean it's any better or worse—that's part of the risk of investing."

5

HOT TIPS
What Stocks to Buy Now

Maybe you've had enough of theories—opinions about what went wrong with the market, why, and how quickly it's likely to recover.

With all that to ponder, you may be looking for something you can act on right away, something you can put to work, something a little less equivocal. What you want, in other words, is tips—hot tips. What are the best stock buys now?

The people who manage portfolios and the analysts who advise them are always—crash or no crash—on the prowl for investment opportunities. They look for industries with good prospects and for strong firms within those industries. And they look for bargains—solid stocks that have been overlooked by other investors.

What you're about to read is up-to-date advice—tips, if you will—from some of the best and the brightest portfolio managers and analysts in the business.

These are the industries, and the companies, that they're going to be looking at in the coming months. You could do worse than to look along with them.

FIRST THINGS FIRST

A couple of notes before you dive in. The stocks mentioned in this chapter are those of the nation's 1,000 largest corporations.

Sales and profit figures are those available as of October 1, 1987. They reflect the most recent year for which complete figures are available.

Finally, a few basic definitions:

A *multiple* is the same as a stock's price/earnings ratio or P/E. What's the P/E? It's simply the price of the stock divided by the company's earnings per share.

There are two types of P/Es: a *trailing P/E*, which is calculated on current earnings, and a *forward P/E*, which uses an estimate of the following year's earnings. For example, a stock that trades for $10 a share and earned $1 a share in 1987 would have a trailing P/E of ten. If its earnings for 1988 are estimated at $2 a share, its forward P/E is five.

The P/E is significant, because it gives investors an idea of how much they're paying for a company's earnings power. The higher the P/E, the more they're paying. Most newspaper stock tables list the trailing P/E.

One last point: Companies listed as "leaders" are among the largest companies in a given industry. Now, here are our experts' favorites.

ADVERTISING

Leaders: Interpublic Group, Ogilvy Group

Experts: Andrew M. Wallach, media analyst, Drexel Burnham Lambert; Alan Gottesman, media analyst, L. F. Rothschild & Co.

Outlook: Positive (for the short term)

Comment: "Before the crash," Wallach says, "I thought that national advertising would grow about 8 to 10 percent in 1988. The three reasons I cited were a sharp improvement in corporate profits, the fact that it's both an Olympic and an election year, and a big surge in new product introductions.

"In light of the crash, I lowered my official estimate of national advertising growth to 7.5 percent in 1988. But I believe we're more likely to see growth of 8.0 percent to 9.0 percent.

"Very few advertising clients and very few agencies have yet felt any effect from the crash in terms of clients cutting back on spending. So the stocks will probably show excellent year-over-year earnings comparisons and excellent earnings growth.

"But," he adds, "my long-run perspective on national advertising is that it will, at best, match the rate of the economy and may even underperform it in certain years.

"Advertising runs in roughly ten-year cycles," Wallach explains. "We've gone through a ten-year period, during which advertising outperformed the economy significantly. But I think starting now and going out ten years, advertising will just match the economy."

"I am cautious in the long run, and I do not think the advertising stocks will be a good investment at all after the middle of 1988."

Comment: "People automatically assume that because there's a recession, advertising will shrink instead of expand," says Gottesman. "They are probably wrong, because in the last couple of recessions, advertising has in fact expanded."

Pick: **Interpublic Group** is one of Wallach's favorites. Based in New York, the company reports sales of $793 million and profits of $41 million. Symbol: IPG. Exchange: NYSE.

Reason: "You pay a little more for Interpublic Group," says Wallach, "but I think it's worthwhile, because of the consistent earnings.

"It's selling for a multiple of around 11 times 1988 earnings, which would put it at a modest discount to the market. And it's a company that has had earnings growth of 17 percent per year per share. Not shabby, but they can't keep it up. I estimate an 11 percent long-term growth rate."

FYI: "If you know any one of the advertising agencies real well," says Gottesman, "you know about 70 percent of all the others. The business is pretty simple."

AEROSPACE

Leaders: Boeing, United Technologies, McDonnell-Douglas

Experts: William N. Deatherage, aerospace industry analyst, Dean Witter Reynolds; Charles I. Clough, Jr., chief investment strategist, Merrill Lynch Capital Markets

Outlook: Mixed

Comment: "Near-term order improvement," says Clough, "and the recent oversold nature of the stocks suggest a rally. The stocks are depressed, and we see selected value in the sector, particularly in the defense electronics stocks."

Pick: Dean Witter's Deatherage is high on **Northrop**. The company, based in Los Angeles, reports sales of $5.6 billion and profits of $41 million.

Reason: "Even in a flat-to-down defense spending environment," Deatherage says, "there are certain companies that can continue to grow. Northrop is one of them, specifically because of its involvement in the advanced technology bomber, or B-2 or Stealth bomber, program.

"B-2," he continues, "already represents 50 percent of Northrop's business. If Stealth goes beyond development into production, it's enough to give the company growth. I'm projecting earnings of $4.15 a share in 1988. The company is selling for a multiple of about 6.4."

Pick: **Martin Marietta** is another buy, Deatherage says. Based in Bethesda, Maryland, the company reports sales of $4.8 billion and profits of $202 million.

Reason: "While Northrop's future hinges on one program, Martin Marietta is diversified," Deatherage says. "But unlike most prime contractors, Martin Marietta doesn't specialize in building aircraft. The company is involved in missile systems, electronic systems, and space systems.

"So when you look at Martin Marietta's product mix, you see that the company has not only opportunities to grow but some safety because of the diversification.

"Martin Marietta," he continues, "is also strong financially. I project earnings of $5 a share for it in 1988, which gives it an earnings multiple of 8."

FYI: "We don't recommend any stock," says Deatherage,

"that we don't think will outperform the market in, say, a 12- to 18-month time horizon."

AIRLINES

Leaders: American Airlines, United Airlines, Delta Airlines

Experts: Charles I. Clough, Jr., chief investment strategist, Merrill Lynch Capital Markets; Helane Becker, airline industry analyst, Shearson Lehman Brothers

Outlook: Negative

Comment: "Stock prices reflect cyclical traffic patterns," Clough reports. "The stocks have broken to a new price low."

Comment: "I never thought the airline industry would do as well traffic-wise in 1988 as it did in 1987," says Becker. "Fares were reasonably priced. Now fares are just slightly too high for airlines to have a repeat of this past summer."

What if the airlines slash fares to boost traffic?

It makes no difference, says Becker. "If traffic is off 5 percent, and fares are off 10 percent, revenues are still going to fall 15 percent."

Pick: Becker rates **Southwest Airlines** a buy. The company, which is based in Dallas, reports sales of $769 million and profits of $50 million.

Reason: "Southwest," Becker says, "has been operating in a recessionary environment in most of their major markets for the last three or four years.

"And," she adds, "they've been doing so profitably.

"They've made some difficult decisions to get out of some markets, liquidate some of their subsidiaries, and focus on Southwest Airlines.

"Southwest is now selling at a discount to book (meaning less than book value)—and at no time in the last 35 quarters have they sold at a discount to book."

FYI: "Most of the airlines are selling at a discount to book," Becker says, "so there are some opportunities in American, Northwest, Delta, and USAir. You buy the stock, trade it up to book value, then sell it. But we recommend this strategy only for aggressive accounts."

ALUMINUM

Leaders: Aluminum Company of America, Reynolds Metals, Kaiser Aluminum & Chemical

Experts: Sean St. Clair, metals analyst, Duff & Phelps Inc.; Peter Anderson, senior vice president, IDS Financial Services; Charles I. Clough, Jr., chief investment strategist, Merrill Lynch Capital Markets

Outlook: Positive

Comment: "We have in North America a natural cost advantage," Anderson says, "because of low-cost power. Also, we're close to our bauxite supplies, which many other smelters in Europe and elsewhere are not.

"Capacity utilization is high. Prices have advanced sharply. Inventories appear relatively low in the hands of users.

"So all of this is a major positive. And, of course, you layer on what happened to the dollar, how it's fallen. I just don't understand," he says, "how smelters in other developed countries can compete, and I think the answer is they can't."

Comment: "The stocks have recovered after a long-term low," Clough reports. "A positive signal for the stocks came two years ago when shipments exceeded production on a year-to-year basis by 20 percent. Inventory liquidation apparently prevented stock-price recovery until now."

Pick: **Reynolds Metals** is St. Clair's pick. Based in Richmond, Virginia, the company reports sales of $3.6 billion and profits of $89 million. Symbol: RLM. Exchange: NYSE.

Reason: "Reynolds," St. Clair says, "has one of the best product lines. They're as close to the consumer as you can get. They actually make the cans. They make the foil.

"They're starting to diversify into other packaging areas. You see this company almost evolving from a pure aluminum company into a specialty packaging company.

"Another kicker you get with Reynolds is that they have some gold mines in Australia. They might spin those off at some stage in the future."

APPLIANCES

Leaders: Whirlpool, Maytag, Chicago Pacific

Experts: Charles I. Clough, Jr., chief investment strategist, Merrill Lynch Capital Markets; Russell Leavitt, appliance industry analyst, Salomon Brothers

Outlook: Negative

Comment: "Credit and growth are beginning to slow," says Clough, "and any latent pickup in demand will likely be short-lived."

Comment: "The sense I have," says Leavitt, "is that consumers are spending somewhat more cautiously than they had prior to the crash. A slowing was already underway before the crash, but the crash may have just speeded up the process."

Pick: None

AUTOMOTIVE

Leaders: General Motors, Ford Motor, Chrysler

Experts: Peter Anderson, senior vice president, IDS Financial Services; Charles I. Clough, Jr., chief investment strategist, Merrill Lynch Capital Markets; Michael M. Luckey, automotive industry analyst, Shearson Lehman Brothers

Outlook: Mixed

Comment: "Auto sales are highly sensitive to the economy," says Luckey, "so when you talk about automobiles, you have to talk about the economy first.

"Our forecast is for slow growth. We have downgraded the forecast since the stock market collapsed. We're talking real GNP growth in the range of 1 to 2 percent.

"But the main reason we forecast slower overall growth is that we expect consumer spending—particularly spending on big-ticket items like cars—will drop in 1988. We think consumer confidence will fall, then probably stay at a low level.

"The problem is not so much the impact of the people who lost a lot of money in the stock market, because most stock ownership is still highly concentrated in the hands of fairly well-to-do individuals. The average person out there doesn't own any stock.

"But the problem is the spillover effect, average people getting a little cautious in their spending, because they're nervous about the stock market signaling tougher times ahead. The stock market is a reasonably reliable leading indicator.

"So sales are likely to weaken in 1988, although they're not going to be as bad as we would see in a recession. Still, the environment is not particularly good for domestic auto stocks—General Motors, Ford, and Chrysler.

"Right now, we're focusing our attention much more on the aftermarket of companies that make replacement parts. The aftermarket is very recession-resistant.

"Even if we were to have a recession in 1988, people are still going to drive their vehicles pretty much the same amount.

"Most driving is essential in nature, not discretionary. The number of vehicles in operation is going to continue to grow.

"This group of used vehicles—vehicles roughly three to seven years old—will generate most of the demand for replacement parts. The number of used cars three to seven years old has been declining for the last several years. By our estimates, however, it's bottoming out now and will grow rapidly over the next couple of years."

Pick: **Ford Motor** is a Luckey favorite. The company, which has its headquarters in Dearborn, Michigan, reports sales of $62.7 billion and profits of $3.29 billion. Symbol: F. Exchange: NYSE.

Reason: "We don't think any of the domestic auto stocks are very attractive," says Luckey, "but we think that one company—Ford—definitely stands out. So for people who think that auto sales may hold up better than we expect, Ford clearly should do the best.

"Their products are still top quality among the domestic companies. They've gained a lot of market share in 1987. We expect that growth to continue. They still have an enormous amount of cash. They've announced a big stock buy-back program. They've raised the dividend by 33 percent.

"So they're doing a lot of things to improve shareholder value, even if auto sales falter."

Pick: **Genuine Parts** is a buy, says Luckey. Based in Atlanta, Georgia, the company reports sales of $2.4 billion and profits of $122 million. Symbol: GPC. Exchange: NYSE.

Reason: "Genuine is a distributor of auto parts," says Luckey. "We're estimating earnings of about $2.25 a share in 1988. So they're selling at a multiple of about 15."

BANKS

Leaders: Citibank, Bank of America, Chase Manhattan

Experts: Charles I. Clough, Jr., chief investment strategist, Merrill Lynch Capital Markets; David Yuschak, vice president and director of research, The Ohio Company; George M. Salem, banking industry analyst, Prudential-Bache Securities; Andrew H. Massie, Jr., managing director, Scudder, Stevens & Clark; Thomas K. Brown, banking industry analyst, Smith Barney, Harris Upham & Co.

Outlook: Mixed

Comment: "Takeover enthusiasm has returned to the regional bank sector," says Clough. "However, regional banks in general are vulnerable to downward pressures on consumer lending margins, and many are exposed to problems related to excessive commercial construction lending.

"Our regional focus," he continues, "remains limited to industrial banks in the Midwest, where year-to-year loan levels are accelerating in response to a better economy. The previously strong New England area could be peaking."

Comment: "While we do not choose to speculate on the impact that the market meltdown will have on the bank acquisition scenario," Yuschak says, "we believe that the market's weakness will segregate the strong banks from the marginal performers.

"Based on our projection that the strongest segment of the economy, the industrial sector, will benefit from the continuing weakness in the dollar, aggressive Midwest regionals should also benefit from increased commercial loan demand."

Comment: Investors are likely to look favorably upon bank stocks in the postcrash environment, Salem concludes.

"We say this based on the following assumptions: Economic growth will be slower, but there will be no recession. Estimates of corporate profits will be scaled back, while bank estimates will be scaled back less or not at all.

"Interest rates will be lower than in previous forecasts and are expected to decline further near term. Revised portfolio strategies will look to groups that can benefit from, or be relatively immune to, this changed economic climate.

"Our endorsement of this group is not a blanket one," he adds. "Whether it is the regionals or the money centers, we would stay with better-quality names. The risks in bottom-fishing don't seem to be worthwhile, since many top-tier names are available at attractive prices.

"A slow-real-growth, declining-interest-rates scenario is positive for bank stocks, but a recession—especially a severe one—would create fear in investors' minds of heavy loan losses and slower loan growth. Our assumption is for no recession in 1988 and roughly 2-percent real GNP growth."

Comment: "I think the country is going to be split into three sections," says Brown. "The banks along the East Coast are slowing. They've been the strongest performers, and, in 1988, I think they're going to be the most uncertain.

"The banks that will be the most consistent and dependable will be those in the Midwest, in the industrial heartland," he concludes. "And those that are going to show the greatest earnings recovery are those west of the Mississippi."

Pick: **BankAmerica** is Brown's top choice. The company, which has its headquarters in San Francisco, reports sales of $12.5 billion and a loss of $577 million. Symbol: BAC. Exchange: NYSE.

Reason: "BankAmerica is the most dramatic turnaround in the banking industry's history," says Brown. "It's already shown four consecutive quarters of improvement.

"Next year, it should have a very solid year in terms of operating earnings and further asset quality improvement. The stock is selling at 3.5 times our 1988 earnings estimate."

Pick: Salem rates **Banc One** a buy. Based in Columbus, Ohio, the company reports sales of $1.8 billion and profits of $194 million. Symbol: ONE. Exchange: NYSE.

Reason: "If a contest were held for the bank with the best financial performance over the last ten years, Banc One would be one of the favorites," Salem says. "For the years 1976 to 1986, Banc One's dividends grew 14 percent per year, and earnings per share grew by 14 percent.

"In addition, Banc One's capital adequacy ranks with the best, and credit quality is good. As investors flee to quality stocks, One has to be a beneficiary."

Pick: Salem also likes Boston-based **Bank of New England**. The company reports sales of $1.9 billion and profits of $167 million. Symbol: BKNE. Exchange: NASDAQ.

Reason: "Either something is wrong," Salem says, "or the present situation represents an excellent opportunity to buy a blue-chip bank stock at a bargain.

"We think the latter is the case. Much of the weakness and low valuation is due to technical stock-trading factors not related to fundamentals. We see a 15 percent-plus earnings growth outlook for 1988 propelled by excellent loan growth, low loan losses, and superior expense control."

Pick: **Barnett Banks** is another Salem favorite. The bank, based in Jacksonville, Florida, reports sales of $1.9 billion and profits of $159 million. Symbol: BBF. Exchange: NYSE.

Reason: "Barnett," Salem says, "is an extremely well-run banking organization that has achieved a growing market share in Florida.

"Despite its aggressive marketing and growth skills, we believe Barnett also has in its culture a conservative lending philosophy. We are not blind to the fact that the U.S. economy is slowing, and Florida historically has had a reputation for a volatile real-estate market.

"In the mid-1970s, Barnett learned its lessons expensively on how not to lend to real-estate developers. Those mistakes will not be repeated," he states.

"The construction portfolio is in good shape today with few

problems. In fact, overall loan quality shows good trends. As of September 30, 1987, nonperforming loans were a mere 1.2 percent of total loans, off from 1.4 percent at midyear."

Pick: Brown is high on **Fleet/Norstar Financial Group** of Albany, New York. The company reports sales of $2.9 billion and profits of $234 million. Symbol: FLT. Exchange: NYSE.

Reason: "Fleet is the most diversified earnings mix of any of the regional banks," says Brown. "It has strong management and excellent asset quality."

Pick: Another Brown favorite is **First Bank System**. The company, which has its headquarters in Minneapolis, reports sales of $2.9 billion and profits of $196 million. Symbol: FBS. Exchange: NYSE.

Reason: "First Bank System is selling at five times our 1988 earnings estimate," says Brown. "The key here is that there has been some investor misunderstanding about the bank's risk profile with respect to interest-rate risk. So what we should see in 1988 is some strong earnings gains driven by a lower loan-loss provision than they had in 1987."

Pick: **First Kentucky National** of Louisville, Kentucky, is one of Massie's favorites. The company reports sales of $478 million and profits of $50 million. Symbol: FKYN. Exchange: NASDAQ.

Pick: Another Massie pick is **First Tennessee National**. The company, which has its headquarters in Memphis, Tennessee, reports sales of $526 million and profits of $47 million. Symbol: FTEN. Exchange: NASDAQ.

Pick: **First Wachovia** is a buy, too, says Salem. Based in Winston-Salem, North Carolina, the bank reports sales of $1.7 billion and profits of $194 million. Symbol: FW. Exchange: NYSE.

Reason: "One of the growing trends among investors after the crash," Salem observes, "is a flight to quality. During uncertain times, investors move to safer, sounder, more reliable companies. First Wachovia is the epitome of this type of stock.

"For over 30 years, it has been recognized as a high-quality, high-performance, conservatively run banking company. Its market territory, North Carolina and Georgia, should outperform the U.S. economy during the next 12 to 18 months.

Pick: Yuschak is high on **Huntington Bancshares**. The company, which has its headquarters in Columbus, Ohio, reports sales of $702 million and profits of $63 million. Symbol: HBAN. Exchange: NASDAQ.

Reason: "As a result of the market meltdown," Yuschak says, "Huntington currently sells at a 7.23 multiple to our 1988 earnings-per-share estimate.

"Huntington represents a bank holding company capable of capitalizing on the strength of its markets. We believe that the current valuation measures afforded Huntington present the investor with an opportunity to purchase a high-quality regional bank at an attractive price."

Pick: Massie's final favorite is **Michigan National** of Farmington Hills, Michigan. The company reports sales of $838 million and profits of $51 million. Symbol: MNCO. Exchange: NASDAQ.

Pick: Salem is high on **Midlantic Corp**. of Edison, New Jersey. The company reports sales of $1.5 billion and profits of $148 million. Symbol: MIDL. Exchange: NASDAQ.

Reason: "Midlantic has a big advantage over its peers in other parts of the United States," says Salem. "Roughly 70 percent of its assets are in New Jersey.

"This (New Jersey's) economic strength manifests itself in such bank fundamentals as high growth, low loan losses, plentiful deposit flows, and above-average earnings.

"The stock," he concludes, "is quite undervalued relative to our universe, and we know of no reason why its multiple is so low."

Pick: **National City** of Cleveland, Ohio, is a Yuschak favorite. The company reports sales of $1.3 billion and profits of $131 million. Symbol: NCTY. Exchange: ASE.

Reason: "We believe that investment in a quality regional bank, such as National City, is prudent in the current market environment," says Yuschak. "As a result of the market retreat,

National City currently sells at a 7.4 multiple to our 1988 earnings-per-share estimate."

Pick: **Norwest** is a buy, says Brown. The company, which has its headquarters in Minneapolis, reports sales of $2.4 billion and profits of $112 million. Symbol: NOB. Exchange: NYSE.

Reason: "Expense reduction from the consolidation of a multistate banking organization and significant asset quality improvement has already started to take place," says Brown.

Pick: Salem's final pick is Pittsburgh's **PNC Financial**. The company reports sales of $2.4 billion and profits of $280 million. Symbol: PNC. Exchange: NYSE.

Reason: "A bank stock investor buys PNC," Salem says, "because it is extremely well managed. It has excellent cost control. Its loan quality is good and stable. It is expanding in a sensible and nondilutive way. Its financial results are among the top 10 percent in banking."

Pick: Brown also rates **SunTrust Banks** high. The company reports sales of $2.5 billion and profits of $244 million. It is based in Atlanta, Georgia. Symbol: STI. Exchange: NYSE.

Reason: "East of the Mississippi," says Brown, "we want to now focus on banks with excellent management and strong asset quality, because we could see deterioration for 1988. That's why SunTrust. It has those characteristics."

Pick: **Wells Fargo** of San Francisco is Brown's final favorite. The company reports sales of $4 billion and profits of $256 million. Symbol: WFC. Exchange: NYSE.

Reason: "Its progress on reducing expenses in the post-Wells Fargo, Crocker acquisition has been fantastic," says Brown.

FYI: All six of his stock picks, Salem says, "are strongly recommended, with comparable appeal and upside potential of 40 percent-plus during the next six months."

BEVERAGES

Leaders: PepsiCo, Coca-Cola, Anheuser-Busch

Experts: Samuel C. Harvey, director, research department,

Hilliard Lyons; Roy D. Burry, beverage industry analyst, Kidder, Peabody & Co.; Henry S. D'Auria, beverage industry analyst, PaineWebber; Douglas M. Loudon, managing director, Scudder, Stevens & Clark

Outlook: Positive

Comment: "Beverages are fairly recession proof," says D'Auria. "People don't change their consumption of soft drinks in a recession.

"That's why these stocks are grouped into a category called defensive stocks. In a period of economic uncertainty, people tend to shift toward companies whose product demand is unlikely to change significantly in a lower-growth environment.

"One of the best examples would be utilities. But beverages are pretty close—right behind utilities. They provide stable and predictable earnings."

Pick: **Coca-Cola** rates a buy, says Loudon. Based in Atlanta, Georgia, the company reports sales of $8.7 billion and profits of $934 million. Symbol: KO. Exchange: NYSE.

Reason: "We're emphasizing the growth or cyclical companies with some foreign exposure," says Loudon. "Coca-Cola is a company with foreign exposure that is reasonably priced."

Pick: D'Auria favors **Coca-Cola Enterprises of Atlanta**, Georgia. The company reports sales of $2 billion and profits of $28 million. Symbol: CCE. Exchange: NYSE.

Reason: "Coca-Cola Enterprises," says D'Auria, "is a bottler that represents about 40 percent of Coke's U.S. volume. It's my favorite pick right now.

"It's selling at a substantial discount to bottling transactions in general. It's currently selling at 6.5 times projected 1988 operating cash flow.

"I see that spread narrowing over the next year."

Pick: **Pepsico** is a buy, says Harvey. The company, which is based in Purchase, New York, reports sales of $9.3 billion and profits of $45 million. Symbol: PEP. Exchange: NYSE.

Reason: "Pepsico is experiencing strong earnings momentum

in each of its three core businesses—soft drinks, snack foods, and restaurants.

"This year," says Harvey, "we anticipate an 18-percent improvement in earnings to $2.60 per share. With its strong consumer brand names, large cash flows, and savvy marketing skills, we believe that Pepsico is an attractive holding for long-term accounts."

Pick: Harvey is high on **Brown-Forman**. Based in Louisville, Kentucky, the company reports sales of $1.1 billion and profits of $89 million. Symbol: BFA. Exchange: ASE.

Reason: "Brand names include Lenox china and Hartmann luggage, and Jack Daniel's, California Cooler, and Canadian Mist," says Harvey.

"Earnings gains could be in the 40- to 45-percent range for the current fiscal year, with earnings-per-share estimated at $3.90.

"Management is superior in our estimation, as are brand recognition levels. We think this stock is an excellent defensive choice for growth-oriented investors."

BROADCASTING

Leaders: Capital Cities/ABC, CBS, Telecommunications

Experts: Alan Gottesman, media industry analyst, L. F. Rothschild & Co.; Charles I. Clough, Jr., chief investment strategist, Merrill Lynch Capital Markets; Andrew H. Massie, Jr., managing director, Scudder, Stevens & Clark; Mara M. Balsbaugh, leisure industry analyst, Smith Barney, Harris Upham & Co.

Outlook: Positive

Comment: "One has to be concerned about the advertising-driven businesses, such as the television-station business," says Smith Barney's Balsbaugh.

"1988 is a tough year to assess, because you've got the elections and the Olympics, which were expected to be a boon to the business. But if we have any kind of economic downturn, I'm reasonably sure you're going to see it accompanied by some softness in advertising.

"So," she concludes, "you may end up with a year that's a wash, rather than any net increment from those two significant events."

Pick: **Capital Cities/ABC** is Gottesman's favorite. Based in New York, the company reports sales of $4.1 billion and profits of $182 million. Symbol: CCB. Exchange: NYSE.

Reason: "Longer term, the relative weakness in Capital Cities is presenting us with a very nice opportunity," says Gottesman. "It's not cheap. It never has been cheap. But I'm looking for something like $15 to $16 a share in earnings in 1987. It could go to $25 a share in 1988."

Pick: Massie favors **Comcast**. The company, which has its headquarters in Bala Cynwyd, Pennsylvania, reports sales of $131 million and profits of $1 million. Symbol: CCPI. Exchange: NASDAQ.

Pick: **Telecommunications** of Englewood, Colorado, is another Massie favorite. The company reports sales of $646 million and profits of $72 million. Symbol: TCOMA. Exchange: NASDAQ.

Reason: "Telecommunications is the largest cable television company in the country, with rapid growth in cash flow," says Massie.

BUILDING MATERIALS

Leaders: Owens-Corning Fiberglas, USG, Jim Walter

Experts: Charles I. Clough, Jr., chief investment strategist, Merrill Lynch Capital Markets; David Yuschak, vice president and director of research, The Ohio Company; Gregory A. Nejmeh, building industry analyst, Shearson Lehman Brothers

Outlook: Negative

Comment: "Building materials order patterns are sluggish," says Clough.

Pick: Nejmeh favors **Sherwin-Williams**. Based in Cleveland, the company reports sales of $1.6 billion and profits of $96 million. Symbol: SHW. Exchange: NYSE.

Reason: "There's a big debate going on now about whether purchases of big-ticket items are going to be hurt by the market crash," says Nejmeh.

"One of the beauties of Sherwin-Williams is that it is a leader in the paint business. People buy paint even during difficult economic times. It's a low-ticket item. Also, painting—even though it's a big pain in the neck—is not tough to do.

"Sherwin has increased its market share in each of the past six years. If you include all its paint brands, it now has about 11 percent of the paint business.

"And since new management took over in 1978, the company has yet to have a down year," he continues. "Earnings are straight up. Today, it has, on top of everything else, $180 million more in cash than in total debt. So it has a highly liquid balance sheet.

"It has bought back stock and will probably continue to do so. Estimates are for earnings of $2.45 in 1988. The stock is selling for a multiple of about ten."

Pick: **Masco** is another Nejmeh favorite. The Taylor, Michigan, company reports sales of $1.5 billion and profits of $203 million. Symbol: MAS. Exchange: NYSE.

Reason: "Masco," Nejmeh says, "is a large diversified company that supplies a number of different items for the home, ranging from faucets to kitchen and bathroom cabinets to plumbing fittings and, most recently, home furnishings.

"Since the summer of 1986, they've made eight acquisitions in home furnishings. Now, their furniture companies will do about $700 to $725 million in revenues in 1988. Masco, by and large, dominates its markets. The company has yet to have a year in which its earnings did not increase.

"The stock is selling at a discount of 19 percent from the market. This is a company that more often than not trades at a fairly hefty premium to the market."

Dissent: "While the results to date are a continuation of the company's outstanding historical performance, the current valuation of this issue reflects uncertainty about future results," Yuschak says.

"Increased exposure in the furniture business and its prospects relative to sluggish consumer spending appear to be investors' main concerns presently.

"As a result, we recommend that investors hold Masco until a clear picture about the economy and the company's ability to manage the economic impact become more apparent."

CHEMICALS

Leaders: Du Pont, Dow Chemical, Monsanto

Experts: Peter Anderson, senior vice president, IDS Financial Services; Charles I. Clough, Jr., chief investment strategist, Merrill Lynch Capital Markets; Theodore S. Semegran, chemicals industry analyst, Shearson Lehman Brothers

Outlook: Mixed

Comment: "Chemical stocks have been in a strong position for more than two and a half years," Clough says. "We think they may be peaking."

Comment: "In an environment of sluggish growth, we'll have earnings in 1988 that are 10 percent to 20 percent higher than earnings in 1987," says Semegran. "The worst case is that earnings will be at 1987 levels."

Pick: **Dow** is a buy, Anderson and Semegran say. The company, based in Midland, Michigan, reports sales of $11.1 billion and profits of $41 million. Symbol: DOW. Exchange: NYSE.

Reason: "The reason we focused on Dow," says Anderson, "is that it's the low-cost producer in many of its lines, and its cash flow and pricing are extremely strong."

Reason: "About 10 percent of Dow's earnings come from drugs and about 10 percent from agricultural chemicals," says Semegran. "Neither is affected by a downturn.

"The company's earnings are going to be somewhere in the neighborhood of $7.50 a share—and that's on a slow-growth case. The stock's multiple is between 10 and 11."

Pick: Semegran also favors **National Distillers & Chemical**. Based in New York City, the company reports revenues of $1.7

billion and profits of $47 million. Symbol: DR. Exchange: NYSE.

Reason: "The company is in excellent shape," says Semegran. "It's operating at 95 to 100 percent of its capacity in most of its product areas."

COMPUTERS AND OFFICE EQUIPMENT

Leaders: International Business Machines, Digital Equipment, Hewlett-Packard

Experts: Samuel C. Harvey, director, research department, Hilliard Lyons; Charles I. Clough, Jr., chief investment strategist, Merrill Lynch Capital Markets

Outlook: Positive

Comment: "Computer stocks have backed off," Clough says, "correcting the first quarter surge. The momentum of orders has slowed but remains positive."

Pick: **IBM** is a buy, says Harvey. The company, based in Armonk, New York, reports sales of $51.3 billion and profits of $4.8 billion. Symbol: IBM. Exchange: NYSE.

Reason: "We are lowering our 1987 and 1988 earnings estimates to $9 and $11, respectively," says Harvey. "Nonetheless, we believe that IBM is the strongest computer company around, and investors desiring to own quality should own IBM."

CONGLOMERATES

Leaders: Tenneco, Rockwell International, Allied-Signal

Experts: Sidney J. Heller, analyst, Shearson Lehman Brothers; Mara M. Balsbaugh, leisure industry analyst, Smith Barney, Harris Upham & Co.

Outlook: Positive

Comment: "A conglomerate is a company that's in lots of different businesses," says Heller. "That diversification should help in a downturn."

Pick: **Figgie International** of Richmond, Virginia, rates high with Heller. The company reports sales of $920 million and profits of $42 million. Symbol: FIGIA. Exchange: NASDAQ.

Reason: "Figgie has done a great job and gets no respect," says Heller. "It has the best return on capital it's ever had. It has a very strong balance sheet. It has tremendous cash flow. It has earnings momentum.

"And despite those facts, the company has had such image problems that the stock sells for about half the market multiple. That's what makes it attractive to me.

"I can't see it going any lower than that, and I think, at some point, it will be at three-quarters of the market multiple, in which case I will have done very well in the stock, without a lot of risk. And it's a stock that's done very well for me in the past.

"The stock is $49, and the company should earn about $7 a share in 1987. So it's selling at about seven times earnings."

Pick: **Gulf & Western** is a buy, says Balsbaugh. The company, which is based in New York City, reports sales of $2.1 billion and profits of $228 million. Symbol: GW. Exchange: NYSE.

Reason: "Gulf & Western," says Balsbaugh, "is gradually shifting from a conglomerate to a media entertainment concern.

"On a price-earnings multiple, it's the cheapest stock in the entertainment group. Unlike Disney or Warner, which trade on midteens multiples, GW trades at ten times earnings.

"And, particularly in an unsettled market, the company's going to get a higher valuation rather than a lower one. So even with no change in the earnings outlook or in the overall market, I think the relative performance of GW could be pretty good."

CONTAINERS AND PACKAGING

Leaders: American Can, Crown Cork & Seal, Ball

Experts: Samuel C. Harvey, director, research department, Hilliard Lyons; Arthur M. Stupay, containers and packaging industry analyst, Prescott, Ball & Turben Inc.

Outlook: Positive

Comment: "The metal beverage can business is strong," says Harvey, "and prospects for continued growth are excellent."

Comment: "The containers and packaging industry will be growing," says Stupay, "because roughly two-thirds of its output is related to the beer and soft-drink industries.

"Soft drinks have a continuous record of growth. In the 1980s, it's been around 5 percent. In a recession or a slowdown, soft-drink consumption doesn't decline, but its rate of growth does fall, usually to the 1- to 3-percent rate.

"The rest of the container demand is related to the food industry. There we have a 1-percent growth that should continue.

"At the same time, overall capacity is expected to rise very slowly, and, indeed, in some parts of the industry, capacity will fall.

"Glass capacity will decline modestly. Can capacity will rise, let's say, 1.5 percent, compared to a 3- to 4-percent rise in demand. Plastics capacity will also be modestly up. So you have growing demand—albeit at a slower rate—and capacity flat to slightly up.

"These conditions should result in higher operating rates throughout the container industries. And we should have somewhat higher prices just on a supply-demand basis. Also, you could have lower raw-material prices. So you could get some help on the cost side.

"So even if the economy does weaken, the container side, the packaging side should do pretty well. We're looking for up earnings."

Pick: **Ball**, which is based in Muncie, Indiana, is a favorite of both Harvey and Stupay. The company reports sales of $1.1 billion and profits of $59 million. Symbol: BLL. Exchange: NYSE.

Reason: "We estimate 20-percent earnings growth for 1988 to $3.05 per share, which would be the twelfth consecutive year of higher earnings," Harvey says. "At eleven times our 1988 estimate, we recommend purchase for capital gains."

Reason: "Ball is a safe stock," says Stupay. "It has little debt, a good earnings outlook, and a continuous record of performance growth."

Pick: **Crown Cork & Seal** is a buy, says Stupay. The company, which has its headquarters in Philadelphia, reports sales of $1.6 billion and profits of $79 million. Symbol: CCK. Exchange: NYSE.

Reason: "Crown Cork & Seal has no debt," says Stupay, "and it generates a lot of cash. They'll earn $9.50 a share in 1988."

Pick: Stupay also likes **Fort Howard Paper**. Based in Green Bay, Wisconsin, the company reports sales of $1.5 billion and profits of $146 million. Symbol: FHP. Exchange: NYSE.

Reason: "Still another safe stock," says Stupay.

FYI: "Three stocks with very high leverage—Anchor Glass, Triangle Industries, and Constar International—are selling for half the market multiple," says Stupay. "But these stocks are only for investors who can tolerate more risk in terms of financial leverage."

DRUGS

Leaders: Merck, Bristol-Myers, Johnson & Johnson

Experts: Charles Allmon, chairman, Growth Stock Outlook Trust; Samuel C. Harvey, director, research department, Hilliard Lyons; David F. Saks, drug industry analyst, L. F. Rothschild & Co.; Charles I. Clough, Jr., chief investment strategist, Merrill Lynch Capital Markets; Douglas M. Loudon, managing director, Scudder, Stevens & Clark; Andrew H. Massie, Jr., managing director, Scudder Stevens & Clark

Outlook: Mixed

Comment: "The drug industry," says Saks, "is poised for continuing record high sales, earnings, and profits. I'm forecasting sales gains of 20 percent in 1988."

Pick: **Baxter Travenol Laboratories** rates a buy, says Loudon. Based in Deerfield, Illinois, the company reports sales of $5.5 billion and profits of $159 million. Symbol: BAX. Exchange: NYSE.

Reason: The stock is reasonably priced, says Loudon.

Pick: Harvey and Loudon are both high on **Bristol-Myers**. The company, based in New York City, reports sales of $4.8 billion and profits of $589 million. Symbol: BMY. Exchange: NYSE.

Reason: "Bristol-Myers is an extraordinarily high-quality company, both in terms of financial strength and the balanced way it generates its operating income," says Harvey.

"Well-known household products and nonprescription pharmaceuticals generate a great deal of excess cash flow, which power a productive pharmaceutical research effort. The combination has produced consistent earnings gains and high returns, and the momentum seems undiminished."

Pick: **Forest Laboratories** is Massie's pick. The company, which has its headquarters in New York City, reports sales of $64 million and profits of $12 million. Symbol: FRX. Exchange: ASE.

Reason: "Forest Labs has grown at a rate of 36 percent a year for the last three years," says Massie. "It should grow at, say, 25 percent over the next three years."

Pick: Loudon also favors **Johnson & Johnson** of New Brunswick, New Jersey. The company reports sales of $7 billion and profits of $330 million. Symbol: JNJ. Exchange: NYSE.

Pick: **Merck** is a buy, Saks says. Based in Rahway, New Jersey, the company reports sales of $4.1 billion and profits of $676 million. Symbol: MRK. Exchange: NYSE.

Reason: "Its (Merck's) momentum is getting stronger," says Saks. "It has been called 'The House that Research Built,' and this research prowess is now breaking out as a driving force propelling the company to record sales, profitability, and earnings growth.

"Together, drugs recently launched and drugs launched in the future will, by our estimates, contribute incremental sales of at least $1 billion by 1988 and $2 billion plus by 1991. And these estimates could prove low.

"Translated into earnings, new pharmaceutical agents could add $3 per share by then, an increment of over 65 percent to 1987's record earnings.

"The 1986 launch of Vasotec for treating high blood pressure and congestive heart failure has been a spectacular success. We project Vasotec sales in 1987 at approximately $620 million, double 1986 levels, and look for that figure to reach $1 billion eventually.

"The recently launched cholesterol lowering agent, Mevacor, may equal or surpass Vasotec's levels. Merck has several other prospective winners in the pipeline.

"We recently increased our earnings projections for 1987, 1988, and 1989 to $6.50, $8.25, and $9.75 per share, respectively."

Dissent: "I think Merck is a great company," says Allmon, "but I won't buy it until it drops 45 percent. It's a fool's paradise. Don't forget the downside of this market is a heck of a lot more than the upside—even though the Dow is off 800 points now."

Pick: **Schering-Plough** is another Saks favorite. The company, which has its headquarters in Madison, New Jersey, reports sales of $2.4 billion and profits of $266 million. Symbol: SGP. Exchange: NYSE.

Reason: "New management has transformed this company into an attractive growth situation. Schering is recovering strongly from a financially depressed period in the early 1980s when it was dependent upon the antibiotic, Garamycin.

"Notable successes," Saks says, "include cardiovascular, dermatological, respiratory, and soft contact lens products. The most exciting potential lies in the recently launched first interferon drug, Intron-A.

"Although now small at about $20 million in annual revenues, Intron-A could evolve into a much more meaningful product as new indications are found for its use as an antiviral drug in treating cancer, AIDS, and other viral infections.

"Recent earnings exceeded expectations, and we are looking for a record $2.70 in 1987, up 24 percent, and tentatively project $3.25, up 20 percent in 1988."

Pick: Saks rates **Squibb** of Princeton, New Jersey a buy, too. The company reports sales of $1.8 billion and profits of $264 million. Symbol: SQB. Exchange: NYSE.

Reason: "Superior results are being recorded in earnings growth, margin expansion, and research productivity," says Saks.

"The company's biggest and fastest selling product is Capoten, the first of a new class of compounds to treat hypertension. Worldwide sales of Capoten in 1987 could exceed $700 million and should surpass $1 billion by 1989.

"Of particular future importance is the development of a cholesterol-lowering drug, Eptastatin. The drug may not be too far behind Merck's similar agent, Mevacor.

"Other attractive attributes are Squibb's very low exposure to generic competition and aggressive endeavors into biotechnology and generics.

"The current P/E at 17.5 times is only a small premium to the drug group and appears reasonable. We find the shares attractively priced."

Pick: **Syntex** is another favorite, says Saks. Based in Palo Alto, California, the company reports sales of $980 million and profits of $207 million. Symbol: SYN. Exchange: NYSE.

Reason: "Syntex is a pure health-care play, generating most of its sales and profit from prescription pharmaceuticals," according to Saks.

"It has been particularly successful in the therapeutic areas of oral contraceptives, analgesics, anti-inflammatories, and dermatology.

"Syntex's most notable recent success is Naprosyn, a medication for the treatment of arthritis, projected to generate worldwide revenues in fiscal 1987 of more than $600 million, greater than 50 percent of total company sales.

"Syntex could benefit greatly from several excellent new drug candidates. New drug approvals are likely in fiscal 1989 for the anti-ulcer agent, Gardrin; the analgesic, Toradol; and the cardiovascular calcium blocker, Cardene.

"Successful new drug launches are critical because exclusive patent protection expires for Naprosyn in 1993," Saks concludes.

ELECTRICAL

Leaders: General Electric, Westinghouse Electric, Emerson Electric

Experts: Samuel C. Harvey, director, research department, Hilliard Lyons; Douglas M. Loudon, managing director, Scudder Stevens & Clark; Russell Leavitt, electrical industry analyst, Salomon Brothers

Outlook: Mixed

Comment: "There is a slowing, a deterioration in the housing part of the industry," says Leavitt. "And consumer debt has reached high levels.

"After October, the impact of reduced wealth, and whatever its effects are on consumer confidence, are likely to cause a decline in product demand. This slowing was already at work, and the crash may have just speeded up the whole process."

Pick: **General Electric** of Fairfield, Connecticut, is a buy, Harvey and Loudon say. The company reports sales of $35.2 billion and profits of $2.5 billion. Symbol: GE. Exchange: NYSE.

Reason: "RCA and several recent acquisitions in financial services have been integrated more quickly than expected," says Harvey.

"The sale of the consumer electronics business and the subsequent purchase in medical technology are viewed as a plus. Ongoing restructuring and the possibility of further acquisitions make GE, in our opinion, a sound long-term investment."

ELECTRONICS

Leaders: Motorola, Raytheon, Intel

Experts: Michael A. Gumport, electronics industry analyst, Drexel Burnham Lambert; Francis J. Saldutti, director of technology research, L. F. Rothschild & Co.; Charles I. Clough, Jr., chief investment strategist, Merrill Lynch Capital markets; Andrew S. Rappaport, president, The Technology Research Group.

Outlook: Mixed

Comment: "Year-to-year order momentum has turned positive," Clough reports.

Comment: "The semiconductor industry," Rappaport says, "is probably the most difficult industry in the U.S. economy to predict with the possible exception of agriculture. The only thing that semiconductors don't have that agriculture does is weather problems.

"If 1988 turns out to be flat as a result of conservative order patterns, there could be a problem for semiconductor companies.

"Carrying semiconductor inventories is extremely expensive for high-technology companies," Rappaport explains. "So most companies watch their inventories extremely carefully, and, in any kind of a downturn, immediately shut off ordering. The last thing you want to have happen, if you're a systems manufacturer, is to be caught with an excess of semiconductor inventories.

"The semiconductor companies, which had massive losses in 1986, are turning profitable again in 1987. But they could go back to periods of massive losses, and that could dramatically affect the stock prices."

Pick: **Amdahl** of Sunnyvale, California, is a buy, says Saldutti. The company reports sales of $966 million and profits of $39 million. Symbol: AMH. Exchange: ASE.

Reason: "Amdahl is winning market share," says Saldutti. "Its cash flow is positive, and it is winning converts in the investment community, which, historically, has shied away from the plug-compatible manufacturers.

"The stock currently sells for about $30, and estimates for 1988 earnings run in excess of $3 a share. Amdahl is selling at no more than ten times 1988 earnings."

Pick: **Intel** is a Gumport favorite. The company, which has its headquarters in Santa Clara, California, reports sales of $1.3 billion and a loss of $183 million. Symbol: INTC. Exchange: NASDAQ.

Reason: "Intel has good sales and earning momentum," says Gumport.

Pick: Saldutti is also high on **Lotus Development** of Cambridge, Massachusetts. The company reports sales of $283 million and profits of $48 million. Symbol: LOTS. Exchange: NASDAQ.

Reason: "Lotus is an interesting company," says Saldutti.

"When IBM introduced the Personal System 2, it also formed a relationship with Lotus, which positions Lotus to become the new member of the inner sanctum with IBM, replacing Microsoft.

"That relationship will give birth over the next twelve months to several major important products from IBM/Lotus."

Lotus is selling for about 15 times 1988 earnings.

Pick: **Motorola** is a buy, says Gumport. The company, based in Schaumburg, Illinois, reports sales of $5.9 billion and profits of $194 million. Symbol: MOT. Exchange: NYSE.

Reason: "Motorola's sales and earnings momentum is good," says Gumport.

Pick: **Tandem Computers** of Cupertino, California, is another Saldutti favorite. The company reports sales of $768 million and profits of $64 million. Symbol: TNDM. Exchange: NASDAQ.

Reason: "Tandem has been, in the short-run, a beneficiary of the crash," says Saldutti. "It was Tandem equipment that allowed some of the stock exchanges to handle the volume they have handled and at the pace they have handled it.

"Tandem remains dominant in the on-line transaction processing businesses. Even in the face of increasing competition from IBM and Digital Equipment, Tandem is generating fast growth and expanding profit margins. And it should be able to do so for some time."

Pick: Gumport also favors **Texas Instruments**. Based in Dallas, Texas, the company reports sales of $5 billion and profits of $28 million. Symbol: TXN. Exchange: NYSE.

Reason: "Texas Instruments doesn't have quite as much value as some of the other stocks such as Avnet and Advanced Micro Devices, but better value than Intel and Motorola," Gumport says. "And TI has very strong momentum and its ongoing business is very strong."

FINANCIAL SERVICES COMPANIES

Leaders: American Express, Merrill Lynch, Salomon Brothers

Experts: Leonard M. Wilson, financial services industry analyst, L. F. Rothschild & Co.; Charles I. Clough, Jr., chief investment strategist, Merrill Lynch Capital Markets; Brenda D. McCoy, financial services industry analyst, PaineWebber

Outlook: Negative

Comment: "Our primary concern has to do with the rapid increase in competition in the industry," says Clough, "and downward pressure on brokerage margins and trading fees."

Comment: "It's going to be a very, very difficult year for financial services," McCoy says. "Overall business is going to slow down significantly from 1986 and 1987 levels.

"The stocks are undervalued. They're trading at multiples we haven't seen since 1974 and 1980. The multiples are half of book value."

Pick: Wilson is high on **American Express**. The company, which has its headquarters in New York City, reports sales of $16.7 billion and profits of $1.1 billion. Symbol: AXP. Exchange: NYSE.

Reason: "American Express is an excellent value," says Wilson. "It's selling right now for $24 a share. We're using an earnings estimate for 1988 of $2.80 to $2.90. At $24, it's selling at about 70 percent of the market multiple.

"It's a complex company, and it's in a number of different businesses. Sixty percent of its earnings are derived from travel-related services—credit cards, traveler's checks, and a data-processing company that's been very successful.

"If we were to give a typical financial services multiple to the financial services business, we calculate that investors would be paying only about nine times earnings for the travel-related portion, and we think that's too cheap. The stock ought to be selling well above the current level."

Pick: **Salomon** is a buy, says McCoy. Based in New York City, the company reports sales of $22.8 billion and profits of $516 million. Symbol: SB. Exchange: NYSE.

Reason: "Salomon has gone through a lot of pain," says McCoy. "The company recently announced it was laying off the equivalent of 12 percent of its staff.

"Salomon had very, very poor earnings results in 1987. The company has taken some dramatic steps to reduce expenses by eliminating head count, getting out of certain businesses that are not profitable, and redirecting its attention and focus to businesses that will maximize returns over a period of years in the future.

"The outlook for the fixed-income market should stabilize in 1988, so we shouldn't see a repetition of the huge trading losses incurred in 1987."

Pick: **Shearson Lehman Brothers** is another McCoy favorite. The company, which has its headquarters in New York City, reports sales of $4.6 billion and profits of $316 million. Symbol: SHE. Exchange: NYSE.

Reason: "Shearson is a bargain," McCoy states flatly.

"It is trading at a very low multiple—about 0.7 times book value. And," she concludes, "it is extremely well managed and very well diversified."

FYI: "You have to realize that you can double your money with these stocks in a month, or you can lose 50 percent in two days. That's how volatile they are," McCoy cautions. "But over the long haul, you'll do all right. These stocks are not for conservative investors."

FOOD PROCESSING

Leaders: Kraft, Sara Lee, Ralston Purina

Experts: Charles I. Clough, Jr., chief investment strategist, Merrill Lynch Capital Markets; John M. McMillin, food industry analyst, Prudential-Bache Securities; Douglas M. Loudon, managing director, Scudder, Stevens & Clark

Outlook: Mixed

Comment: "Unless farm products fall a lot further," says Clough, "peak margin gains have probably been seen."

Comment: "People eat in good economic times and bad," says McMillin. "So the industry isn't significantly influenced by economic activity.

"Earnings trends continue in the lower double-digit rate on a pretax basis. And these companies should be able to maintain those kinds of rates.

"This group of stocks," McMillin continues, "is selling at only 11 times earnings. The market is selling at a higher multiple. It seems to me that, during these times, the defensive quality of packaged food companies will make the stocks shine."

Pick: **Campbell Soup** is a buy, says McMillin. The company, based in Camden, New Jersey, reports sales of $4.5 billion and profits of $247 million. Symbol: CPB. Exchange: NYSE.

Reason: "We're in an environment now where the companies with strong balance sheets do better," McMillin says. "Campbell Soup has an exceptionally strong balance sheet."

Pick: McMillin likes **Dean Foods**, too. Based in Franklin Park, Illinois, the company reports sales of $1 billion and profits of $32 million. Symbol: DF. Exchange: NYSE.

Reason: "Lower milk prices in combination with a consolidating dairy industry makes this stock attractive," McMillin says.

Pick: **Gerber Products** of Freemont, Michigan, is another McMillin favorite. The company reports sales of $917 million and profits of $37 million. Symbol: GEB. Exchange: NYSE.

Reason: "The company," McMillin reports, "is now fully recovered from the glass scare."

Pick: **H. J. Heinz** is a buy, McMillin and Loudon say. The company, which has its headquarters in Pittsburgh, Pennsylvania, reports sales of $4.6 billion and profits of $338 million. Symbol: HNZ. Exchange: NYSE.

Reason: "Earnings grow like clockwork," McMillin says.

Pick: McMillin also favors **Kellogg**. The company reports sales of $3.3 billion and profits of $319 million. It is based in Battle Creek, Michigan. Symbol: K. Exchange: NYSE.

Reason: "Kellogg is another company with a strong balance sheet," McMillin notes. "And it represents a flight to quality."

Pick: McMillin likes **Kraft**, too. The company, which has its headquarters in Glenview, Illinois, reports sales of $8.7 billion and profits of $390 million. Symbol: KRA. Exchange: NYSE.

Reason: "Kraft is a company that has had a disappointing track record," says McMillin. "But it's on track now."

FYI: "I have a bias toward those companies with strong balance sheets," says McMillin. "They're in a position to buy back more of their own stock. Also, in times of economic uncertainty, companies with higher balance sheets historically get a higher multiple.

"In the last couple of years," he adds, "it's actually been the more-leveraged companies that have gotten the higher price/earnings multiples, partly due to their ability to get better returns by using leverage. I think that game has now stopped."

GENERAL MACHINERY

Leaders: Ingersoll-Rand, Sundstrand, Timken

Experts: Charles I. Clough, Jr., chief investment strategist, Merrill Lynch Capital Markets; Douglas M. Loudon, managing director, Scudder, Stevens & Clark; Barry A. Mannis, machinery industry analyst, Shearson Lehman Brothers

Outlook: Mixed

Comment: "Order momentum in the industrial and construction sectors now shows modest signs of acceleration," says Clough.

Comment: "The market," Mannis says, "is operating within a recessionary framework, so I'm trying to look at the industry within that same framework.

"The heavy-duty truck market was already starting to come off its peak. The anticipation of a recession, whether we have one or not, means that the industry will come off that cyclical peak a little more quickly than it otherwise would.

"Other sectors of the industry are continuing to see good orders—for example, manufacturers of component parts. So I think we're going to see some strength continue in that area until companies are sure there's going to be a recession.

"Remember, too, that a lot of these companies are beneficiaries of the lower dollar. They're still seeing increased demand because of better price competitive positions versus the overseas people who have killed them for the last ten years.

"They're finally getting some of that back, and they're going to keep chugging along until the last minute. They've been waiting for this one.

"Next, I think the expansion into construction equipment is going to be very short-lived and not very pronounced. These stocks have been strong performers since the crash, and I think the expectations are a little high if we do get a recession."

Pick: **Caterpillar** rates high with Loudon. The company, which has its headquarters in Peoria, Illinois, reports sales of $7.3 billion and profits of $76 million. Symbol: CAT. Exchange: NYSE.

Pick: **Navistar International** is a buy, Mannis says. Based in Chicago, the company reports sales of $3.4 billion and a loss of $16 million. Symbol: NAV. Exchange: NYSE.

Reason: "Navistar is my favorite," Mannis concludes, "because Navistar is the leader in the industry in terms of market share."

Pick: **Mack Trucks** is a buy, too, Mannis says. The company, which has its headquarters in Allentown, Pennsylvania, reports sales of $1.7 billion and a loss of $35 million. Symbol: MACK. Exchange: NASDAQ.

Pick: **PACCAR** is another Mannis favorite. Based in Bellevue, Washington, the company reports sales of $1.8 billion and profits of $54 million. Symbol: PCAR. Exchange: NASDAQ.

Reason: "PACCAR has financial strength," Mannis says. "It has a solid balance sheet, and it's not completely dependent on the heavy-duty truck market."

Pick: Mannis is also high on Cleveland-based **Eaton**. The company reports sales of $3.8 billion and profits of $137 million. Symbol: ETN. Exchange: NYSE.

Reason: "Eaton Corp. is a supplier of components for heavy-duty trucks," Mannis says. "Its other primary market is the control business, which has been strong lately."

FYI: "My rationale for Mack, Navistar, and PACCAR is very similar," Mannis explains. "They're all three primarily assemblers of heavy-duty trucks.

"The strength of orders that we've seen over the past year and a half will translate into strong earnings over the next couple of quarters, because the backlog has been built up very high. These companies will see appreciation based on strong earnings.

"It's as straight a cyclical story as you could get. We've seen the orders. I know the earnings are in backlog. The stocks all moved quite well during the strong earnings period, and I'm anticipating that they'll move again when the earnings come."

HOMEBUILDING

Leaders: Pulte Home, U.S. Home, Kaufman & Broad

Expert: Charles I. Clough, Jr., chief investment strategist, Merrill Lynch Capital Markets

Outlook: Negative

Comment: "Homebuilding stocks," Clough reports, "have dropped to a new relative price low. We've never really had much of an up cycle over the past three years."

Pick: None.

INSURANCE

Leaders: Aetna Life & Casualty, Cigna, Travelers

Experts: Charles Allmon, chairman, Growth Stock Outlook Trust; Samuel C. Harvey, director, research department, Hilliard Lyons; Leonard M. Wilson, financial services industry analyst, L. F. Rothschild & Co.; Charles I. Clough, Jr., chief investment strategist, Merrill Lynch Capital Markets

Outlook: Mixed

Pick: Allmon likes **American Family Life**. The company, which has its headquarters in Columbus, Georgia, reports sales of $1.4 billion and profits of $78 million. Symbol: AFL. Exchange: NYSE.

Reason: "American Family sells cancer insurance. Two thirds of its net income is derived from the sale of cancer insurance in Japan," Allmon says. "The company was listed in late 1987 on the Tokyo stock exchange, and I would expect the P/E multiple to go substantially higher."

Pick: **Capital Holding** is Harvey's pick. Based in Louisville, the company reports sales of $2.3 billion and profits of $148 million. Symbol: CPH. Exchange: NYSE.

Reason: "Capitol Holding has one of the most impressive track records in the industry with 17 consecutive years of earnings and dividend increases," says Harvey.

"CPH has been among the leading innovators in the industry through its direct marketing life and health insurance subsidiary. Its pace of innovation in other facets of the business has been somewhat slower and even deliberate, therefore minimizing risk.

"We look for a full year earnings gain to $3.30 a share from $2.92 per share. A further gain in 1988 to $3.65 a share appears reasonable."

INSTRUMENTS

Leaders: Johnson Controls, General Signal, Tektronix

Experts: Douglas M. Loudon, managing director, Scudder, Stevens & Clark

Outlook: Mixed

Pick: Loudon favors **General Signal**. Based in Stamford, Connecticut, the company reports sales of $1.6 billion and profits of $75 million. Symbol: GSX. Exchange: NYSE.

LEISURE TIME INDUSTRIES

Leaders: Eastman Kodak, Walt Disney, Warner Communications

Experts: Mara M. Balsbaugh, leisure industry analyst, Smith Barney, Harris Upham & Co.

Outlook: Positive

Comment: "I'm not overly concerned about any real fallout in the box-office business and the cable television business," says Balsbaugh.

"Both those areas have shown tremendous resilience in economic downturns. And certainly you're not talking about major discretionary income, spending to go out to a movie or to keep your cable subscription. So I think in those areas I'm relatively sanguine.

"I am concerned about the theme park business. That certainly is something that people would put off if they're not overly optimistic about the economy or if they're in a saving mode. That obviously would have implications for Disney.

"There are some mitigating factors—like the baby boomlet. Also, if the dollar stays low, you'll have a lot of foreign visitors.

"In the music area, where we've seen a lot of growth in the last year, I think there is some indication that sales of CD players are slowing down.

"It's not clear whether this juncture is a temporary glitch or if, in fact, we've saturated the audiophiles, and CDs have gone as far as they're going to go. If that's true," Balsbaugh says, "I'd certainly be worried about the record companies.

"Also, the recent industry developments, such as Sony's purchase of CBS Records, probably doesn't bode well for the record companies, particularly if you get some price cutting on compact disks in order to pave the way for the introduction of digital audio tape.

"Typically, music sales are not necessarily a victim of a downturn. However, when the market is driven by hardware sales—sales of CD players—it could well be."

Pick: Balsbaugh is bullish on **Tri-Star Pictures**. Traded over-the-counter, the company, based in New York City, reports sales of $254 million and profits of $14 million. Symbol: TRSP. Exchange: NASDAQ.

Reason: "Tri-Star Pictures is going to merge with Coke's Columbia unit. Both of these studios will continue to be operated separately but under the same corporate roof.

"But the big part of that story," Balsbaugh says, "is you now have an opportunity to run Columbia properly, which it has not been for the last couple of years.

"And both these studios—Tri-Star and Columbia—have had their worst years ever at the box office. And in my experience, that's the time to buy film companies."

Pick: **Disney** is another of Balsbaugh's picks. The company, which has its headquarters in Burbank, California, reports sales of $2.5 billion and profits of $247 million. Symbol: DIS. Exchange: NYSE.

Reason: "We still like Disney for the long term," Balsbaugh says, "although I'm somewhat cautious about the theme parks."

LODGING

Leaders: Marriott, Holiday, Hilton Hotels

Experts: Charles I. Clough, Jr., chief investment strategist, Merrill Lynch Capital Markets; Joseph J. Doyle, lodging industry analyst, Smith Barney, Harris Upham & Co.

Outlook: Mixed

Comment: "Periodic takeover rallies have been buoying stock prices," Clough says, "but downward pressure on room rates has continued to threaten profit margins."

Comment: "The business is sensitive to the economic cycle," Doyle notes, "but we're not looking for a recession. Demand is good for the hotel business. In fact, if anything, it's better than expected since the crash.

"On the supply side, the outlook is brightening as well. The industry has been characterized by overbuilding in the last four or five years," he continues.

"Now, you're seeing a decline of 20 to 25 percent in new hotel construction starts in 1987. And I think these declines should continue for the next two to three years."

Pick: **Marriott** is first on Doyle's buy list. Based in Washington, D.C., the company reports sales of $5.3 billion and profits of $192 million. Symbol: MHS. Exchange: NYSE.

Reason: "Marriott is one of the best-managed companies in America—in any industry," says Doyle. "It is also a growth company. Over the past seven years, Marriott has gone from about a 25,000-room system to about a 70,000-room system.

"The company continues to build new hotels, including different brands for different segments of the business. It is now building a middle-priced concept—in the $60-a-night area—by the name of Courtyard. It's building about 40 Courtyards a year, and there are about 80 of them now.

"Marriott is also building Residence Inns. Residence Inns is a company that it purchased in July 1987. There are more than 100 Residence Inns in operation, and the company will build about 35 to 40 of those a year. That is a suites-only concept.

"The target for Residence Inns is the extended stay market—where someone has to be in a town for a week, two weeks, whatever. If you're going to be there a month, it's one price. If you're going to be there a week, it's another price.

"Courtyards and Residence Inns run at occupancy rates of about 80 percent, which is exceptionally good, since the industry average is only 65 to 66 percent.

"Marriott stock is at the low end of its historical P/E range," Doyle says. "We have a $2.10 earnings estimate for 1988, so the stock is selling for about 14 times earnings.

"That's a 15-percent premium to the market. But," he adds, "Marriott, over the past five years, has traded at a 50-percent premium to the market."

Pick: **Hilton** is Doyle's second choice. The company, based in Beverly Hills, California, reports sales of $719 million and profits of $98 million. Symbol: HLT. Exchange: NYSE.

Reason: "Hilton is not a growth story," says Doyle, "although there are new Hiltons being built, and there is some growth.

"Hilton is primarily an earnings turnaround story. Earnings have been stuck at around $4 a share from 1980 through 1986. You're finally going to see an improvement. Earnings will be $4.40 a share in 1987 and $5.15 in 1988.

"Hilton is also an asset value story," he continues. "The company owns several very valuable hotels, including the Waldorf Astoria in New York."

METALS AND MINING

Leaders: Newmont Mining, Homestake Mining, AMAX

Experts: Sean St. Clair, metals and mining industry analyst, Duff & Phelps; Charles Allmon, chairman, Growth Stock Outlook Trust; Peter Anderson, senior vice president, IDS Financial Services; Charles I. Clough, Jr., chief investment strategist, Merrill Lynch Capital Markets

Outlook: Mixed

Comment: "I'm not sure I'd buy gold itself," says St. Clair, "but I think it *is* time to buy gold stocks. There are some interesting opportunities out there."

Pick: **Newmont Mining** is a favorite of St. Clair and Allmon. Based in New York City, the company reports sales of $381 million and profits of $69 million. Symbol: NEM. Exchange: NYSE.

Reason: "Newmont is the premier North American gold mining company," says St. Clair. "It will be the largest producer of gold in North America probably for the next four to five years, producing a million ounces plus of gold a year."

Reason: "Newmont Mining is the classic gold stock in this country," says Allmon. "We've owned it for over a year, and it's up over 250 percent. I'm not complaining. I think the big push in gold shares is yet to come."

FYI: "Copper capacity in this country," Anderson observes, "has been chopped and chopped mercilessly. So what is left in the copper industry are extremely efficient copper producers. All the inefficient producers have basically been shut down.

"We are seeing an increase in demand. Inventories are low. And, given low inventories and rising demand and declining capacity, we've seen an increase in prices. As a result," he concludes, "the earnings of these companies are exploding."

MISCELLANEOUS MANUFACTURING

Leaders: Minnesota Mining & Manufacturing, PPG Industries, Borg-Warner

Experts: Samuel C. Harvey, director, research department, Hilliard Lyons

Outlook: Mixed

Pick: Harvey is high on **Herman Miller**. The company, based in Zeeland, Michigan, reports sales of $574 million and profits of $33 million. Symbol: MLHR. Exchange: NASDAQ.

Reason: "Herman Miller," Harvey says, "is the leader in the office furniture industry and it's growing at four to six times the industry. The company is expanding its product lines with stronger products at the low end of the price scale and exciting innovative products at the upper end.

"Earnings growth should come from market share gains resulting from the expanded product line and enhanced distribution system. Finances are conservative, and we look for earnings to increase 34 percent to $1.80 per share in 1988. The stock sells at 10.6 times our earnings estimate."

Pick: **Kimball International** is a buy, says Harvey. Based in Jaspar, Indiana, the company reports sales of $394 million and profits of $26 million. Symbol: KBALB. Exchange: NASDAQ.

Reason: "Kimball International is a well-disciplined and well-capitalized company with the bulk of its earnings derived from office furniture and electronics assemblies.

"Earnings," Harvey says, "could reach $3.80 per share for the fiscal year ending June 30, 1988, for an increase of 35 percent over 1987.

"Kimball holds cash of $49 million and has a debt-to-capital ratio of 8 percent, a very important strength in difficult times. The P/E ratio is a low ten times our fiscal year 1988 estimate. A recent two-for-one split was paid to holders of record on November 6."

Pick: **Stanadyne** of Windsor, Connecticut, is another Harvey favorite. The company reports sales of $493 million and profits of $21 million. Symbol: STNA. Exchange: NASDAQ.

Reason: "We are attracted to its Moen Group plumbing supply subsidiary, one of the largest manufacturers of single-handled faucets," says Harvey. "The Moen Group's pretax operating return on assets was an exceptional 51 percent in 1987.

"We look for a strong earnings rebound to $3.50 per share for Stanadyne in 1987, up nearly 60 percent from 1988's depressed $2.20."

Stanadyne sells for about 7.5 times 1988 earnings.

OIL AND NATURAL GAS

Leaders: Exxon, Mobil, Chevron

Experts: Charles I. Clough, Jr., chief investment strategist, Merrill Lynch Capital Markets; Sanford L. Margoshes, oil industry analyst, Shearson Lehman Brothers

Outlook: Mixed

Comment: "Oil stocks have moved up persistently," says Clough. "We believe a major bottom was made. Our investment focus is on the domestic producers."

Comment: "My outlook is somewhat more sanguine than most other observers," says Margoshes. "For example, I believe that oil prices, while likely to weaken this spring, are going to weaken from a level higher than we're at currently.

"The official OPEC price is $18, with spot prices about $15. We could see some modest recovery between now and spring, followed by some further erosion.

"Despite weakness in crude pricing, oil companies will show healthy cash flows in 1988, partly due to better refining margins. Net income will typically be flat to up 5 percent.

"An increase in the price of oil would enhance incentives for exploration, but the lower crude price is not helping at the moment. It would probably mean, from a market standpoint, that the oils are not likely to outperform the market, unless the market itself declines visibly.

"I'm looking for an upside surprise."

Pick: **Exxon** is a buy, says Margoshes. The company, based in

New York City, reports sales of $69.9 billion and profits of $5.4 billion. Symbol: XON. Exchange: NYSE.

Reason: "We're recommending Exxon for long-term investors. It has the highest sustainable rate of return on equity of any of the major oils.

"It is very cost conscious," Margoshes adds. "It has the lowest long-term debt to total capital, which increases its flexibility should anything interesting come along. And it has a policy of buying its own stock when doing so is the most advantageous use of its capital."

PAPER AND FOREST PRODUCTS

Leaders: Weyerhaeuser, Georgia-Pacific, International Paper

Experts: Peter Anderson, senior vice president, IDS Financial Services; Charles I. Clough, Jr., chief investment strategist, Merrill Lynch Capital Markets; Lawrence A. Ross, paper and forest products industry analyst, PaineWebber

Outlook: Mixed

Comment: "We've normally been the world's low-cost producer of paper," says Anderson, "and when I say we, I'm including the Canadians.

"In the early 1980s, that fact was obscured by the tremendous strength of the dollar. With the collapse of the dollar, that natural cost advantage is reasserting itself.

"Paper exports are booming," he concludes. "Capacity utilization in the paper industry is sky high. We've already seen two or three rounds of price increases, and it looks like we're going to get several more."

Comment: "Paper prices are likely to rise a bit longer," Clough says. "Given the maturity of the cycle, and the fact that capacity utilization and price momentum are decelerating, our model is negative."

Comment: "The paper industry," Ross says, "will have an earnings gain of at least 15 to 18 percent in 1988. We're forecasting approximately a 4-percent increase in product prices, a 1-percent increase in volume, and a 3-percent increase in costs.

"Also, we're scheduled to have a 6-percentage point reduction in corporate taxes. The corporate rate is going from 40 percent to 34 percent. According to our estimates, this reduction adds about 7 percent to the earnings of the industry.

"In addition, we have a dollar that is continuing to decline, and that has historically been quite an important factor for the paper industry. North America is a big exporter. So the dollar is helpful in the industry's profitability."

Pick: **Federal Paper Board** is a buy, says Ross. Based in Montvale, New Jersey, the company reports sales of $949 million and profits of $26 million. Symbol: FBO. Exchange: NYSE.

Reason: "At a time of economic uncertainty," Ross says, "we like to concentrate on companies that have interesting internal programs that are designed to increase profitability. Federal is that kind of a company.

"We think its mill program, which it's just finishing, could add between $1.10 and $1.20 a share to its annual earning power starting in 1989.

"Also, Federal has a good product mix. The company is currently earning $4 per share. Using our estimate for next year," Ross says, "Federal's stock is selling for between eight and nine times earnings."

Pick: Ross also rates **Great Northern Nekoosa** a buy. The company, which has its headquarters in Stamford, Connecticut, reports sales of $2 billion a year and profits of $85 million. Symbol: GNN. Exchange: NYSE.

Reason: "Great Northern," Ross says, "is a producer of market pulp, liner board, newsprint, and uncoated white paper—the best parts of the industry to be in.

"We think the company will earn $4.40 a share next year—and it may do better than that. The multiple is between nine and ten."

Pick: **Weyerhaeuser** is another Ross favorite. Based in Tacoma, Washington, the company reports sales of $5.7 billion and profits of $248 million. Symbol: WY. Exchange: NYSE.

Reason: "Weyerhaeuser," Ross says, "is the largest exporter in the industry. So it is very strong right now. The multiple on the stock is between nine and ten."

PERSONAL CARE PRODUCTS

Leaders: Procter & Gamble, Colgate-Palmolive, Avon Products

Experts: Charles Allmon, chairman, Growth Stock Outlook Trust; Samuel C. Harvey, director, research department, Hilliard Lyons

Outlook: Mixed

Pick: Allmon likes **Clorox**. The company, based in Oakland, California reports sales of $1.1 billion and profits of $96 million. Symbol: CLX. Exchange: NYSE.

Reason: "Here's one you can really clean up with," says Allmon. "Its P/E multiple is 12.7 based on estimated earnings for 1988. It's just a good steady company, but there's a potential take-over play there also."

Pick: **International Flavors & Fragrances** is a buy, says Harvey. Based in New York, the company reports sales of $621 million and profits of $86 million. Symbol: IFF. Exchange: NYSE.

Reason: "We think of International Flavors & Fragrances as something of a miniature Coca-Cola, with a myriad of proprietary chemical formulae," Harvey says.

"While none is as valuable as the Coke formula, many ingredients for fine perfumes, soaps, foods, beverages, and all sorts of other items are manufactured by International Flavors & Fragrances. Business momentum is strong and persistent dollar weakness inures to IFF's benefit."

POLLUTION CONTROL

Leaders: Waste Management, Chemical Waste Management, Rollins Environmental Systems

Experts: Andrew H. Massie, Jr., managing director, Scudder, Stevens & Clark; Barry A. Mannis, pollution control industry analyst, Shearson Lehman Brothers

Outlook: Positive

Comment: "My outlook is bright all around," says Mannis. "Pollution control—particularly the solid waste business—is about the best place I can think of to be in a recession."

"Growth in the industry, which has been very strong to date, has been driven primarily by two factors. These are a continued shortage of suppliers of services and capacity of services to handle and—even more so—dispose of wastes, and the fact that growth is being driven by an increasing regulatory environment that is making more and more stringent the practices that can be used in handling waste.

"On the solid waste, or garbage, side, the greater impact is coming from shortage of capacity; on the hazardous waste side, the greater driver is the regulatory trends.

"My recession scenario calls for the solid-waste industry to be impacted less than the hazardous-waste industry.

"After all, garbage is only a function of you and I continuing to throw things out, and we'll continue to do so in a recession at a very similar pace. But hazardous waste, at least to some extent, depends on manufacturing and industrial activity.

"My annual growth rate for the solid-waste industry outside of a recession is about 20 to 23 percent a year for the next five years. My recession scenario calls for closer to 18- to 20-percent growth a year.

"On the hazardous waste side, outside of a recession, I'm looking for 30- to 35-percent growth, and in a recession more like 25- to 28-percent growth. The drop-off is bigger but the absolute growth still remains higher."

Pick: **Ogden** is a buy, says Massie. The company reports sales of $800 million and profits of $38 million. It is based in New York City. Symbol: OG. Exchange: NYSE.

Pick: Massie also rates **Rollins Environmental Services** high. The company, which has its headquarters in Wilmington, Delaware, reports sales of $137 million and profits of $19 million. Symbol: REN. Exchange: NYSE.

Pick: Mannis lists **Waste Management** as his favorite. The company, based in Oak Brook, Illinois, reports sales of $2 billion and profits of $371 million. Symbol: WMX. Exchange: NYSE.

Reason: "My single favorite stock across the board is Waste Management," he says. "The company is a leader on both sides of the industry. And therefore you're maximally playing both sides of the waste business by owning its shares.

"It's also the largest company in the business, and, in this type of market environment, the safest place to have your money. It was beaten down, but because the company is recognized as a leader in such a high-growth market, it's come back quite well.

Pick: **Combustion Engineering** of Stamford, Connecticut, is a buy, says Mannis. The company reports sales of $2.6 billion and profits of $56 million. Symbol: CSP. Exchange: NYSE.

Reason: "I like Combustion Engineering as a developing play," Mannis explains. "Its traditional strength is in the boiler market.

"But it has also developed a very strong position in the process controls business. Combustion is now the leading supplier of process controls systems and software for the pulp and paper industry, which for the last couple of years has been operating at over 95-percent capacity utilization.

"As for the power systems market, over the next five to ten years we're not looking for any kind of sharp upturn, but for a gradually increasing pace of spending by utilities on retrofit and maintenance of existing plants.

"Forecasts indicate that by the mid-1990s the excess reserve margins that electric utilities carry will be getting quite tight. And that means a lot of brownouts.

"So they'd be retrofitting additional capacity onto existing plants, adopting, say, more frequent maintenance schedules to make sure they keep the plants up and running maximally.

"Since Combustion Engineering originally installed so many of these systems, it's now going back and doing all that maintenance and retrofit work. And the profitability on this type of work is much greater than on selling equipment."

PUBLISHING

Leaders: Dun & Bradstreet, Gannett, Times Mirror

Experts: Alan Gottesman, media industry analyst, L. F. Rothschild & Co.; Charles I. Clough, Jr., chief investment strategist, Merrill Lynch Capital Markets; Andrew H. Massie, Jr., managing director, Scudder, Stevens & Clark

Outlook: Mixed

Comment: "You have to be very careful about publishing," says Gottesman, "because there are a couple of different sectors, and they behave differently.

"Take the newspaper companies," he continues. "Newspapers are the predominant local advertising medium in the United States. And a very important part of a newspaper's business is classified advertising. It can be 20 or 30 percent of advertising revenues.

"Classified advertising depends on used jobs, used cars, and used houses. And all those tend not to be advertised very heavily during a recession.

"Retail advertising may be subject to retailers' reactions. So a lot of newspapers have had an unusual degree of cyclicality.

"But magazine companies may be strong in 1988, because the national advertising scene will probably do okay."

Pick: **Gannett** is a buy, says Massie. Based in Arlington, Virginia, the company reports sales of $2.8 billion and profits of $276 million. Symbol: GCI. Exchange: NYSE.

Reason: "Gannett gets most of its earnings from small suburban newspapers that are typically insensitive to economic trends," says Massie.

"And it's benefiting from the growth of *USA Today*, which I think will continue despite what the economy does. So I think Gannett is a good bet."

Pick: **The Washington Post** is another winner, says Massie. The company, which has its headquarters in Washington, D.C., reports sales of $1.2 billion and profits of $100 million. Symbol: WPOB. Exchange: ASE.

Reason: "*The Washington Post* is very well managed," says Massie. "And the Washington market is much more sensitive to political trends than economic trends. So I think it'll sail right through any recession."

RAILROADS

Leaders: Burlington Northern, Union Pacific, CSX

Experts: Charles I. Clough, Jr., chief investment strategist, Merrill Lynch Capital Markets; James A. C. Kennedy III, vice president and director of equity research, T. Rowe Price Associates

Outlook: Positive

Comment: "The rail industry has cut costs and written down unproductive or overvalued assets," Clough says. "It is highly profit-leveraged into any pickup in industrial production and rail-car loadings. These stocks should continue to perform better."

Pick: **Burlington Northern** of Seattle, Washington, is one of Kennedy's favorites. The company reports sales of $6.9 billion and a loss of $558 million. Symbol: BNI. Exchange: NYSE.

Reason: "Burlington is cheap on a price-to-cash flow basis," Kennedy says. "It has a lot of upside potential on an asset basis."

Pick: **Union Pacific** is another Kennedy favorite. The company, which is based in New York City, reports sales of $6.6 billion and a loss of $445 million. Symbol: UNP. Exchange: NYSE.

Reason: "Union Pacific," Kennedy notes, "is selling at the lowest P/E ratio than it's been at in over a decade. Again, it has a tremendous underlying asset base."

RESTAURANTS

Leaders: McDonald's, Wendy's International, Shoney's

Experts: Samuel C. Harvey, director, research department, Hilliard Lyons; Charles I. Clough, Jr., chief investment strategist, Merrill Lynch Capital Markets; Joseph J. Doyle, senior vice president, Smith Barney, Harris Upham & Co.

Outlook: Negative

Comment: "Owing to signs of a peaking in restaurant sales momentum," says Clough, "our word is negative."

Comment: "We don't think the events of October will trip us into a recession," Doyle notes. "With that as a preface, we expect that the restaurant business outlook for 1988 is pretty much what we thought it would be a couple of months ago—sluggish.

"This sluggishness is related to the two ongoing problems in the restaurant business. First, you still have overbuilding. You have too many restaurants out there chasing too few consumer dollars for eating out. And, second, you have sluggish demand for eating out."

Pick: **McDonald's** is one of Doyle's favorites. The company, which is based in Oak Brook, Illinois, reports sales of $4.1 billion and profits of $476 million. Symbol: MCD. Exchange: NYSE.

Reason: "McDonald's is the dominant company in the industry," says Doyle. "It has proven in the past that it can get through recessions very nicely.

"The other dimension at McDonald's—which no other restaurant company has—is that its foreign business is doing well and growing at a healthy rate.

"About 20 percent of its business is now overseas, and it's growing about 20 percent a year," he continues. "The domestic business is growing at about 10 percent a year.

"So combining the foreign and the domestic businesses, McDonald's could grow at 13 to 14 percent a year, a very healthy number. We've got a $3.40 earnings estimate on the company in 1988. So it's trading at about 13 times earnings."

Pick: Doyle rates **Shoney's** a buy. So does Harvey. Based in Nashville, Tennessee, the company reports sales of $623 million and profits of $42 million. Symbol: SHON. Exchange: NASDAQ.

Reason: "Shoney's is probably the best-managed company in the family restaurant business," says Doyle. "It's very attentive to the details.

"Shoney's sales experience, unlike McDonald's, was soft in 1987," he continues. "The company is trying to turn that around."

Doyle's earnings estimate for the company is $1.70 a share in

1988. It's now selling for about 13 times earnings. "This is the first time in six or seven years that Shoney's has traded at such a small premium to the market," he notes.

Reason: Harvey agrees with Doyle's assessment. "We view Shoney's as one of the best-managed, consistently successful companies in the restaurant business," he says.

"The company has recorded higher sales and pretax earnings each quarter for more than 27 years. Earnings for fiscal 1988 should be up 26 percent. We regard current prices as an excellent opportunity to build positions in Shoney's," he concludes.

RETAILING

Leaders: Sears, Roebuck, K Mart, J. C. Penney

Experts: Robert F. Buchanan, retailing industry analyst, L. F. Rothschild & Co.; Charles I. Clough, Jr., chief investment strategist, Merrill Lynch Capital Markets; Andrew H. Massie, Jr., managing director, Scudder, Stevens & Clark; Stacy Ruchlamer, retailing industry analyst, Shearson Lehman Brothers

Outlook: Mixed

Comment: "The outlook for retailing is poor the first half of the year," says Buchanan. "The second half of the year is really anyone's guess.

"But we're looking at the year as a whole as poor to fair. I think we will continue to experience sluggish growth in real disposable income next year.

"So people will be in less of a buying mood in light of sluggish growth in real disposable income, low savings rates, and also high personal debt levels."

Comment: "The earnings disappointments reported by a number of specialty retailers," Clough says, "may be symptomatic of the risk of a coming margin squeeze."

Comment: "Starting in the spring of 1987, consumers began to slow down in their purchasing," says Ruchlamer. "They were spent out, tired.

"Their savings had diminished. Their debt levels had built. Their real weekly earnings had dramatically declined, especially versus inflation.

"Also, prices were going up, and there was a lack of newness and excitement in the fashion. A lot of stores looked the same.

"On September 21, we took all our buys off every retail stock.

"Inventories had begun to build. So we thought we would now have a promotional environment, and that would hurt profits.

"That's really what's going on right now. And going into the first half of 1988, we suspect the consumer is going to slow down spending even more. So I'm not looking for anything stellar in the first half of 1988."

Pick: **Dress Barn** is a buy, says Massie. Based in Stamford, Connecticut, the company reports sales of $136 million and profits of $9 million. Symbol: DBRN. Exchange: NASDAQ.

Reason: "It's a very well-managed company that has had impressive long-term growth rates," says Massie. "The stock has been destroyed, yet, when the dust settles, I think it will again reassert itself as a leader."

Pick: **K Mart** is a Ruchlamer favorite. The company, which has its headquarters in Troy, Michigan, reports sales of $24 billion and profits of $570 million. Symbol: KM. Exchange: NYSE.

Reason: "K Mart, like Wal-Mart, is a leader in the low end of the spectrum," says Ruchlamer. "It also has sales and earnings momentum."

Pick: **Melville** is a Buchanan favorite. The company, which has its headquarters in Harrison, New York, reports sales of $5.3 billion and profits of $238 million. Symbol: MES. Exchange: NYSE.

Reason: "Melville is a diversified specialty retailer," says Buchanan. "My earnings estimates are $4.90 a share in 1987 and $5.60 a share in 1988.

"It's trading at a discount to the market. And I like the business mix. About 60 percent of its sales are generated by two divisions that I think would be resistant in a recession—CVS, a drug store chain, and Marshall's, an off-price apparel store chain."

Pick: Massie also favors **Pic 'n Save** of Carson, California. The company reports sales of $303 million and profits of $40 million. Symbol: PICN. Exchange: NASDAQ.

Reason: Massie likes Pic 'n Save for the same reasons he likes Dress Barn—it's well managed and has an impressive record of growth.

Pick: Buchanan favors giant **Sears, Roebuck**. The company, which has its headquarters in Chicago, Illinois, reports sales of $44.3 billion and profits of $1.3 billion. Symbol: S. Exchange: NYSE.

Reason: "Sears will do fine in 1988 given the strength in Allstate insurance, which today is perhaps the largest single contributor to company earnings. The outlook for general merchandise at Sears, I think, is fair," Buchanan says.

"The stock is trading at a multiple of seven times 1988 earnings," he concludes. "So it's selling at a big discount to the market."

Pick: Ruchlamer is a fan of **Wal-Mart Stores**. So is Massie. Based in Bentonville, Arkansas, the company reports sales of $11.9 billion and profits of $450 million. Symbol: WMT. Exchange: NYSE.

Reason: "I'm looking to recommend those companies that have good sales and earnings momentum, that are selling basic, not fashion, merchandise, and that are known to have good value and good quality," says Ruchlamer. "Wal-Mart is in that vein."

Dissent: "I'm very high on Wal-Mart as a company," says Buchanan. "The company has done very little wrong over the last ten years.

"But I also think that the stock is trading at a huge premium to the market. It's like walking into a grocery store and buying a box of cornflakes. I like the cornflakes at $1 a box. But I don't like them at $2 a box."

FYI: "Retail stocks are the first to go down before a recession," says Ruchlamer, "and they're the first to go up after a recession."

SAVINGS & LOAN

Leaders: Great Western Financial, H. F. Ahmanson, CalFed

Experts: Charles I. Clough, Jr., chief investment strategist, Merrill Lynch Capital Markets

Outlook: Negative

Comment: "Savings and loan stocks have been in a long relative price downtrend," says Clough. "Many of the large savings and loans have built a large percentage of adjustable rate mortgages (ARMs) into the asset base. This may protect spreads, but one often-expressed concern is that spreads may deteriorate."

Pick: None

SERVICE INDUSTRIES

Leaders: Federal Express, Ryder System, Hospital Corporation of America

Experts: Samuel C. Harvey, director, research department, Hilliard Lyons; Andrew H. Massie, Jr., managing director, Scudder, Stevens & Clark

Outlook: Mixed

Pick: Harvey likes **New England Business Service** of Groton, Massachusetts. The company reports sales of $1.4 billion and profits of $172 million. Symbol: NEBS. Exchange: NASDAQ.

Reason: New England Business "is a high-quality growth company with outstanding earnings," says Harvey. "The company should earn $1.45 to $1.50 in calendar-year 1988. In our opinion, NEBS is an excellent buy at fourteen times calendar 1988 earnings."

Pick: **Service Corporation International** is a buy, says Massie. Based in Houston, Texas, the company reports sales of $387 million and profits of $52 million. Symbol: SRV. Exchange: NYSE.

Reason: "Service Corporation provides funeral services," says Massie. "The company has shown a remarkably stable growth rate in recent years—15 percent a year in the last three years. It's going to accelerate in the next three years to about 18 percent a year."

STEEL

Leaders: USX, Bethlehem Steel, Inland Steel Industries

Experts: Peter Anderson, senior vice president, IDS Financial Services; Charles I. Clough, Jr., chief investment strategist, Merrill Lynch Capital Markets; David Yuschak, vice president and director of research, The Ohio Company.

Outlook: Mixed

Comment: "The steel industry has cut its costs and cut its capacity," Anderson says. "We've seen such a collapse of the dollar that our steel production costs are now lower than those in Japan and Europe. Once again, we're competitive in the world market."

Comment: "Steel stocks have rallied from a severely oversold condition, as have most industrials," Clough says.

Pick: **USX** is Anderson's choice. Based in Pittsburgh, Pennsylvania, the company reports sales of $14 billion and a loss of $1.7 billion. Symbol: X. Exchange: NYSE.

Reason: "With the collapse of the dollar, once again, these guys can compete," Anderson says. "USX is the strongest company in the steel industry. It's only a partial steel play, because it also has a large oil component, Marathon Oil. Marathon has tremendous reserve strength."

Pick: **Worthington Industries** is a buy, says Yuschak. The company, based in Columbus, Ohio, reports sales of $819 million and profits of $42 million. Symbol: WTHG. Exchange: NASDAQ.

Reason: "Worthington Industries is well-positioned to take advantage of manufacturing opportunities in this country," Yuschak says.

"Not only do we expect it to increase penetration of existing markets, but to broaden its product lines through internal development, as well as through acquisition.

"We believe the common stock of this well-managed manufacturing company is headed for a period of overperformance relative to the market."

TELECOMMUNICATIONS

Leaders: American Telephone & Telegraph, GTE, BellSouth

Experts: Elizabeth M. Shiels, telecommunications industry analyst, Hilliard Lyons; Charles I. Clough, Jr., chief investment strategist, Merrill Lynch Capital Markets; Jack B. Grubman, telecommunications industry analyst, PaineWebber; John S. Bain, telecommunications industry analyst, Shearson Lehman Brothers

Outlook: Positive

Comment: "The telecommunications industry is going to do well for two reasons," says Grubman. "Regulation is becoming more and more relaxed, both at the federal and the state level, which means that the major telephone companies will be earning more money.

"And there is no evidence that there is any slow-up in the growth of telephone usage, particularly among business users.

"So a combination of increased network usage and less regulation will translate into better profitability for the major telephone service providers.

"And even if there is a recession, the telephone industry will grow, not as much as it might, but it will still grow.

"Telephone usage is fairly economically insensitive. So, putting it all together, in a medium-to-good economy, the telephone industry should do very well with very good growth. In a bad economy, the industry will still grow, although maybe at a more moderate level."

Comment: "Based on the extraordinarily strong performance of the telephone companies since the October 19 crash, the market's perception appears to be that the telephone industry, as a public utility, is less susceptible to a downturn than the business sector in general," says Bain.

"So investors with a defensive attitude toward the general economy should consider the local exchange telephone companies as components of a recession-resistant portfolio of common stocks."

Pick: **American Telephone & Telegraph** is a buy, says Grubman. The company, which has its headquarters in New York City, reports sales of $34.1 billion and profits of $228 million. Symbol: T. Exchange: NYSE.

Reason: "AT&T is the dominant player in this industry," says Grubman, "so it's the biggest beneficiary of more growth and less regulation.

"With AT&T, you have a strong balance sheet, strong financial condition, a big franchise, and the prospects of earnings momentum coming out of less regulation of its long-distance business.

"I think it is going to be one of the best performing stocks over the next year," Grubman concludes. "It has all the attributes you want in a nervous market—it's big and blue-chip, yet there is a story emerging as regulation becomes less.

"I have a $2.10-a-share earnings estimate for 1988 and a $2.60 estimate for 1989. The stock is selling at roughly a 5- to 6-percent premium to the market. It should eventually sell at a 15- to 20-percent premium, given all its qualities."

Pick: **BellSouth** is Shiels' favorite. Based in Atlanta, Georgia, the company reports sales of $11.4 billion and profits of $1.6 billion. Symbol: BLS. Exchange: NYSE.

Reason: "BellSouth has the advantage of strong population growth, advanced technology throughout the system. And it's the best positioned for growth of the group," says Shiels. "The current yield is 5.9 percent.

"We expect earnings to reach $3.80 per share in 1988. Earnings and dividend growth could exceed 7 percent a year over the next five years."

Pick: Bain likes **Southwestern Bell** of St. Louis, Missouri. The company reports sales of $7.9 billion and profits of $1 billion. Symbol: SBC. Exchange: NYSE.

Pick: Grubman also rates **United Telecommunications** high. The company reports sales of $2.9 billion and profits of $183 million. It is based in Kansas City, Missouri. Symbol: UT. Exchange: NYSE.

Reason: "United Telecommunications is roughly two-thirds local independent telephone companies, and one-third Sprint," says Grubman. "United Telecom, along with GTE, owns one-half of U.S. Sprint, which is a competitor to AT&T long-distance.

"I view United Telecommunications as a high-yielding (7.5 percent) telephone utility with an earnings turnaround story. Sprint is still losing a lot of money, but I expect it to turn around by the end of 1988.

"We've seen the first evidence of a turnaround in the third quarter, which, unfortunately, got lost in the shuffle of the crash.

"As Sprint goes from losing $800 million in 1987 on a pretax basis, to, say, losing $150 million in 1988, United Telecom's earnings will go from a loss of 50 cents to $2.60 in earnings for 1988 and $3.50 in earnings for 1989. And there are very few telephone utilities with a 7.5 percent yield where you can see earnings quadruple over a two-year period.

"So you get the best of both worlds. You get a high-yielding company for current income. But you also get the very real prospects of a big earnings story.

"Once Sprint is at breakeven, United Telecom stock will be selling in the high $30 to $40 a share. It's currently at $25 a share."

Pick: Shiels rates **US West** high. And so does Bain. The company, based in Englewood, Colorado, reports sales of $8.3 billion and profits of $924 million. Symbol: USW. Exchange: NYSE.

Reason: "US West appeals to us because of its yield (6.6 percent), its solid earnings potential, and the appeal of the spinoff of its cellular telephone business. The growth rate is modestly lower than BellSouth," says Shiels, "but the difference in yield offsets that. USW has the lowest payout ratio of the operating companies, leaving room for somewhat better near-term dividend growth."

FYI: "Since the crash," says Bain, "the telephone companies have been absolutely fantastic performers—up 30 to 40 percent versus the broad market averages.

"And in the crash itself, the Dow was down 23.6 percent, the S&P 500 was down 22.8, but the regional Bell holding companies as a group were down only 11.2."

TEXTILES AND APPAREL

Leaders: Liz Claiborne, VF, Reebox International

Experts: Charles I. Clough, Jr., chief investment strategist, Merrill Lynch Capital Markets; Andrew H. Massie, Jr., managing director, Scudder, Stevens & Clark; Stacy Ruchlamer, retailing industry analyst, Shearson Lehman Brothers

Outlook: Negative

Comment: "Textile mill production continues to decelerate even in the face of import restrictions and a lower dollar," says Clough. "We think profit margins will erode for this industry in coming quarters. The stocks are in a downtrend."

TOBACCO

Leaders: Philip Morris, RJR Nabisco, American Brands

Experts: Roy D. Burry, tobacco industry analyst, Kidder, Peabody & Co.; Henry S. D'Auria, tobacco industry analyst, PaineWebber; and Diana Temple, tobacco industry analyst, Salomon Brothers

Outlook: Positive

Comment: "In an environment where you have slower growth," says D'Auria, "these are defensive stocks. People don't smoke less in a recession. There's sometimes a shift within smoking to more value-priced categories. But the overall consumption isn't affected much."

Pick: D'Auria rates **Philip Morris** high. The company, which has its headquarters in New York City, reports sales of $20.7 billion and profits of $1.5 billion. Symbol: MO. Exchange: NYSE.

Reason: "Philip Morris is a market leader," says D'Auria. "It has the ability to increase prices at substantially higher rates than inflation. People continue to smoke despite about 8- to 10-percent increases annually in the cost of cigarettes."

Pick: **RJR Nabisco** is a buy, says D'Auria. Based in Atlanta, Georgia, the company reports sales of $16 billion and profits of $978 million. Symbol: RJR. Exchange: NYSE.

Reason: "RJR still gets about 70 percent of its operating income from the tobacco area," says D'Auria, "despite its purchase of Nabisco."

FYI: "Initially," says D'Auria, "it seemed Congress would solve some of the budget deficit questions by increasing excise taxes. Now, it seems Congress is taking the position that excise taxes are regressive—not the type of revenue enhancements it's looking for."

TRUCKING

Leaders: Consolidated Freightways, Roadway Services, Yellow Freight System

Experts: Samuel C. Harvey, director, research department, Hilliard Lyons; Burton M. Strauss Jr., trucking industry analyst, E. F. Hutton & Co.; Craig A. Kloner, trucking industry analyst, Goldman, Sachs & Co.; and Charles I. Clough, Jr., chief investment strategist, Merrill Lynch Capital Markets

Outlook: Mixed

Comment: "The trucking industry is in the process of consolidation," Kloner says. "You have some companies going out of business. And more of them are going to go out of business, whether there's a recession or not. It's a function of deregulation.

"Even before the crash, trucking stocks dramatically underperformed the market.

"Quite frankly, with bankruptcies in the industry, consolidation, and fewer competitors, the industry's earnings, for the major carriers, are going to go up. And I would expect that the trucking stocks will reflect that improvement in profitability."

Comment: "The industry," Strauss says, "has gone through a period in the last twelve months of heavy rate competition. This competition has diminished for now.

"We're looking at earnings that are 30 to 65 percent greater than in 1987. These earnings are based on our outlook for the economy, but they aren't expected to be adversely affected by the crash."

Pick: **Consolidated Freightways** rates high with Strauss. The company, which has its headquarters in Palo Alto, California, reports sales of $2.1 billion and profits of $89 million. Symbol: CNF. Exchange: NYSE.

Reason: "We're staying with companies that are financially the strongest," says Strauss. "Consolidated Freightways is one of those companies."

Pick: **Roadway Services** is a buy, says Harvey. Based in Akron, Ohio, the company reports sales of $1.7 billion and profits of $76 million. Symbol: ROAD. Exchange: NASDAQ.

Reason: One reason Roadway Services is attractive, Harvey says, is that the company has $7.50 per share in cash and no debt. "We believe pricing pressures in the industry are easing," he says, "paving the way for improved earnings. We think $2.50 per share is possible in 1988."

Pick: **Yellow Freight System** of Overland Park, Kansas, is a favorite of Strauss. The company reports revenues of $1.7 billion and profits of $67 million. Symbol: YELL. Exchange: NASDAQ.

Reason: "Yellow Freight is another financially strong company," says Strauss.

UTILITIES

Leaders: PacificCorp, Southern, Commonwealth Edison

Experts: Charles I. Clough, Jr., chief investment strategist, Merrill Lynch Capital Markets; David Yuschak, vice president, director of research, The Ohio Company.

Outlook: Positive

Comment: "Relative to the market," Clough reports, "utility stocks have suddenly rallied sharply to the upside."

Pick: **American Electric Power** rates a buy, says Yuschak. Based in Columbus, Ohio, the company reports sales of $4.8 billion and profits of $507 million. Symbol: AEP. Exchange: NYSE.

Reason: "American Electric Power, long an underperforming utility, is well positioned to take advantage of deregulation through its transmission capabilities," says Yuschak.

Pick: **Kentucky Utilities** is favored by both Clough and Yuschak. The company, based in Lexington, Kentucky, reports sales of $551 million and profits of $54 million. Symbol: KU. Exchange: NYSE.

Reason: "Kentucky Utilities' scaled-back construction program is having a very positive effect on its free cash flow," says Yuschak. "Its stronger balance sheet and building investment portfolio should support above-average dividend growth."

Pick: Yuschak rates **Oklahoma Gas & Electric** a buy. Based in Oklahoma City, Oklahoma, the company reports sales of $1.1 billion and profits of $119 million. Symbol: OGE. Exchange: NYSE.

Reason: "Oklahoma Gas & Electric's strong financial condition and low construction budget should bode well for future dividend increases," Yuschak says. "Earnings will also be aided by a cost-containment program. OGE is an excellent utility for the conservative investor."

Pick: **PacificCorp** is another Yuschak favorite. Based in San Francisco, California, the company reports sales of $7.8 billion and profits of $925 million. Symbol: PPW. Exchange: NYSE.

Reason: "PacificCorp is continuing on-track in the proposed merger with Utah Power & Light (UPL). The company is currently awaiting the approval of the Utah Public Utility Commission.

"PacificCorp," Yuschak says, "expects the merger to be completed by the end of the second quarter of 1988, barring any entanglements from competitors about antitrust infringement. Its competitors consist of independent power producers, who have yet to intervene in the merger proposal.

"We feel the merger will be very beneficial to both concerns," he concludes. "It will help eliminate the surplus of power currently available in that region, enabling PacificCorp to reduce excess operating expenses and further boost profits."

Pick: **Public Service Enterprises** is a favorite of Clough and Yuschak. The company reports sales of $4.5 billion and profits of $378 million. It is based in Newark, New Jersey. Symbol: PEG. Exchange: NYSE.

Reason: "Public Service Enterprises' financial condition is also improving after commercial operation began at its Hope Creek facility," Yuschak says.

"As a result, its free cash flow should be on a solid upswing. We look for the company to spend some of that extra cash in its nonregulated businesses."

Pick: **Southern Indiana Gas & Electric** is another Clough and Yuschak favorite. The company, which has its headquarters in Evansville, Indiana, reports sales of $269 million and profits of $30 million. Symbol: SIG. Exchange: NYSE.

Reason: "Southern Indiana Gas, one of the industry's best-managed companies, is well positioned to generate above-average dividend growth," says Yuschak.

"A favorable regulatory climate, solid returns on equity, and a relatively small construction budget bode well for this company's continued success."

Pick: Clough and Yuschak like **Teco Energy** of Tampa, Florida. The company reports sales of $902 million and profits of $98 million. Symbol: TE. Exchange: NYSE.

Reason: "Teco Energy is a solid investment for those investors looking for superior dividend growth," says Yuschak. "Improved results of the company's coal mining unit, plus off-system sales, are benefiting earnings. Its transportation unit is also performing quite well."

FYI: "While in recent years we have traditionally favored utilities in the growth regions of the South and West, as well as issues in favorable regulatory climates, these criteria may not be as successful in an environment of deregulation," says Yuschak.

"Deregulation, by definition, means less dependence on regulatory control and more dependence on market conditions. We believe that market conditions are becoming increasingly more favorable for the rust belt of this country.

"As a result, our list of recommended utilities is dominated by power companies in that region. For the most part, these utilities are centrally located in the heart of the country where an important part of our industrial growth will reestablish itself."

FYI: "While investment dollars can be earned speculating in troubled nuclear-related utilities," says Yuschak, "the time period to resolution has been so inexact that money can be lost just as easily when important deadlines to completion are not met."

6

GIVE ME LAND
The Outlook for Real Estate

Let's face it. There's a solidity to real estate that no paper asset—certificate of deposit or bond, for instance—can match. It has an esthetic dimension that no newspaper stock table can capture and report. But is it a good investment?

When the financial markets turn upside down, is real estate the high ground or the swamp? Do you really want to own it? Where? And how?

In this chapter, you'll learn what the experts see ahead for the real-estate market. They'll tell you which parts of the country are hot—and which are not.

Hint: Their answers may surprise you.

You also get the pros and cons on various real-estate investment vehicles. For example, you may find that a real-estate investment trust and real-estate limited partnership are better buys for you than a single apartment building, say.

OUR EXPERTS

Our panel of experts on real estate are:

- Robert A. Frank, real-estate industry analyst for Alex Brown & Sons, investment bankers in Baltimore, Maryland.
- Monte Helme, vice president of Century 21 Real Estate, which has its international headquarters in Irvine, California.
- Arthur J. Hill, chairman and chief executive officer of the Coldwell Banker Real Estate Group, based in Chicago.
- Barry A. Greenfield, vice president of Boston-based Fidelity Investments and manager of the Fidelity Real Estate Investment Portfolio.
- Kenneth Danter, president and founder of Kenneth Danter & Co., a real-estate research firm based in Columbus, Ohio.
- John S. Moody, president and chief executive officer of PaineWebber Properties, which has its headquarters in New York City.
- Roger C. Hindman, personal financial planning partner, the Consumer Financial Institute (CFI) in Waltham, Massachusetts. CFI is a division of Price Waterhouse.

Here's what our experts had to say.

How did the market's meltdown affect real estate?

Moody: "The impact of the crash on real estate is positive, not negative. There are going to be more investment dollars flowing into real estate.

"People who are scared by the volatility of the stock and bond markets are going to hedge their positions a little and reallocate some of their assets to real estate.

"Some people may view real estate differently after the crash. But the business itself—and the yields people can expect—are the same."

Hill: "I definitely don't see a real-estate crash. Indeed, investors may show renewed interest in investments such as real estate that act as hedges to inflation.

"Pension funds now have 3 percent or more of their assets in real estate. We believe many are moving toward the 5- to 10-percent range.

"Of course, in Manhattan—a place that is sensitive to the fortunes of the securities industry—office leasing could slow. And prices for condos and co-ops could soften."

Danter: "Some clients are taking a wait-and-see attitude as far as new projects are concerned. Other clients say they believe the market collapse may bring fresh money into the real-estate business. So the crash may bring good news for real estate."

Say more money does flow into real estate. Will the money come from individuals or institutions?

Moody: "The money will come from both individuals and institutions. The big institutional money—the billions of dollars will probably go to direct ownership, although some of it may go to managed accounts at the big financial institutions.

"But I see more money trying to find a home in real estate in 1988—and I'm talking industry-wide—than we had in 1987."

Will demand outstrip supply?

Moody: "It's going to be tough. It's going to get crowded. Everyone, and that includes the foreigners, is looking for institutional-grade real estate. There's only a finite supply of that kind of property, so you're going to see some pressure on supply."

Hill: "Foreign demand, from both the Japanese and Europeans, continues very strong. Yes, there is a shortage of investment-grade properties for sale."

What is investment-grade property?

Moody: "Office buildings, shopping centers, and apartments in major metropolitan markets qualify as investment- or institutional-grade real estate.

"Some people might disagree with me about apartments, but there are only eight to ten major metropolitan areas in the United States.

"We don't go into cities where there are only 50,000 people, because we might have trouble finding a buyer when we get ready to sell."

Will foreign demand for U.S. real estate continue?

Greenfield: "I think so.

"Everyone talks about the Japanese, but the Europeans have been buying up real estate in the United States like crazy. In fact, the Japanese aren't big buyers of real estate, though we see a lot of megadeals. But very quietly the Europeans are buying up a lot of commercial real estate.

"And foreign demand wasn't affected by the stock-market crash. Those people aren't in it to get rich quick. In Germany people buy buildings where they get no return at all. They put in a million dollars and get no income. They're just there for the appreciation.

"The Japanese buy buildings to make a 4-percent return on their money. Americans have traditionally looked for a 7- to 15-percent return.

"So when foreigners look at this country, it looks cheap. Now, with the dollar having collapsed since October 19, U.S. commercial real estate is going to look even cheaper to foreigners. And if you and I don't want to buy it, they will.

"They may think twice about buying Merck or General Electric after the crash, but they'll go in and buy a downtown office building in Philadelphia just like that, particularly since they're buying it with appreciated deutsche marks or appreciated yen.

"So I'm extremely bullish on real estate because of the foreign factor. I'm also bullish because the tax law took the wise guys out of the game. And real estate is a safe bet. If you bought real estate any time during your lifetime and just hung on, sooner or later it came through.

"But there are some stocks that never come back."

In the old days, people could expect their property to appreciate 10 to 20 percent a year or more. Will we see those kinds of returns again?

Moody: "In the late 1970s, real estate did appreciate 10 percent to 20 percent a year or more if you added in cash flow. But those days are over."

Hill: "For many people, a home has been far and away their best investment. But it would take some price inflation to match the more dramatic gains of the past."

So where are real estate prices heading?

Moody: "It depends on the economy. If there's a possibility of deflation—and I don't think there is—real-estate prices may drop.

"But if the economy grows, the stock market stabilizes, and corporate earnings increase, then demand for real estate will increase, rents will increase, and the amount people will pay for property will increase. That's what I think is going to happen."

How did the outlook for real estate change when Congress adopted the 1986 Tax Reform Act?

Hindman: "Congress made the depreciation rules less favorable to investors. Under the old depreciation schedules, you could deduct from your taxable income each year for 19 years a portion of the cost of your investment property.

"The 1986 tax law stretched out to 27.5 years the amount of time it takes to recoup your investment in apartments and other residential rental property. Depreciation schedules for commercial real estate, such as office buildings, run even longer—31.5 years.

"The 1986 law also eliminated the use of accelerated depreciation, which allowed you to garner larger write-offs in the early years of ownership.

"You must now use less generous straight-line depreciation. With straight-line depreciation, write-offs remain the same from year to year."

What other rules changed?

Hindman: "Under the 1986 tax law, you may deduct so-called passive losses only from passive income. And income from rental property qualifies as passive income. Income from limited partnerships also counts as passive income.

"The rule means that expenses you pile up when you rent property—depreciation, utility bills, and so on—are deductible only from your passive income. If you report no passive income, you may not write off your passive losses at all.

"You may, however, carry any losses you can't deduct currently forward to future years and write them off then, when you report passive income.

"The law does allow a phase-in period for this new rule. If you made your rental investment before October 22, 1986, and you put the building in service by December 31, 1986, you may still deduct a portion of your losses from your regular income until 1990.

"You may write off 65 percent of your passive rental losses in 1987, 40 percent in 1988, 20 percent in 1989, and 10 percent in 1990.

"The law does provide a number of exceptions to the passive-loss rules to help moderate-income investors. For example, the law says you may deduct rental losses up to $25,000 from your regular income under two conditions: You meet the income requirements, and you actively participate in the operation of your rental property.

"You're entitled to write off up to $25,000 in rental losses from your regular income if your adjusted gross income (AGI) is $100,000 or less.

"If your AGI falls between $100,000 and $150,000, another rule applies. You reduce the $25,000 limit by 50 percent of the amount your AGI tops $100,000. Say your AGI is $110,000. You subtract $5,000—that is, $10,000 times 50 percent—from the $25,000 limit. Therefore, you may deduct $20,000 in rental losses.

"If your AGI exceeds $150,000, you may not deduct a cent of your rental losses from your regular income. You must deduct these losses only from your passive income.

"Now let's go on to the other test—active participation. To write off your losses from your regular income, you must participate in the property's management.

"That means you own at least a 10-percent stake, and you make the decisions that count—setting rental terms, signing off on expenditures, and so on."

What's the long term outlook for real estate?

Greenfield: "Real estate was a tax shelter. And, as a result, we went on a building binge from 1981 to 1986. We didn't care what we built as long as there were write-offs.

"Well, that's stopped. Now the country is growing into its

excess inventory of real estate. Take apartment buildings as an example.

"No one is building apartment buildings. So as the apartment buildings fill up, the landlords are going to raise the rent to the tenants. They're going to start to squeeze the tenants.

"Then it will become profitable for someone to go out and build a new apartment building because rents are so high. And they'll build real estate for economic reasons, not tax reasons.

"The bottom line: I see tremendous growth coming in real estate. I think there's a coming boom because of the changes in the tax law.

"My time frame is 1991, 1992. Existing real estate will start to appreciate when we work off the glut of 1981 to 1986.

"The last thing to appreciate will be office buildings, because that's where the greatest glut is. But apartment buildings, nursing homes, substance-abuse centers, shopping centers, and grocery stores—we're going to need all of these sooner rather than later."

Moody: "The money that's flowing into real estate is all for existing buildings now. You don't have money going into new construction, the highly speculative product.

"But that's good news, not bad. You've cut off the supply spigot. So, if this trend continues, in time, the oversupply problem will correct itself.

"If the economy stays strong and the demand for new space continues to grow, you will have more buyers than sellers, and prices will firm."

What's the outlook for real estate in 1988?

Hill: "I look for a solid but unspectacular year, barring a significant recession. The market would slow if there's a recession."

Is now the time to invest in real estate?

Frank: "We think there's currently a window of opportunity. But we're suggesting that investors shift their thinking from location, location, location, to location, location, management.

"We're moving from an era of investing in real estate as individual properties to investing in real estate as a diversified managed portfolio."

What advice would you give real-estate investors in the wake of the market crash?

Hill: "Buy quality. Buy real estate where you understand the property and the neighborhood. Don't get overleveraged—and have ample staying power.

"Also, don't let the stock-market crash change your residential game plan. If you're planning to sell, seek a full market price. Slashing prices in today's environment would, in my opinion, be an outright mistake."

Moody: "Look for areas, such as the East and West coasts where land is scarce and zoning is strict. That way, you have something with intrinsic value. You have a protected franchise, because you know there will only be so many new units added to your market each year."

Frank: "Make sure your real-estate investment matches your investment objectives. Make sure you're not in an aggressive speculative deal unless you want to be."

Greenfield: "Be patient. Investors today are very impatient. People buy major office buildings and sell them six months later.

"I was down in Palm Beach looking for a house and found one where people had put money down, the property appreciated, and they wanted to sell the contract on the house.

"We've trained the whole world that way with instant drive-in windows for McDonald's or one-hour cleaning. And we invest that way, too. But this is one area of investing—whether it's before the crash or after the crash—where people can't have instant gratification.

How much of an investor's portfolio should be allocated to real estate?

Greenfield: "No one should have all their money in real estate. But everybody should have a little—maybe 5 to 10 percent of a portfolio."

Let's talk about what's hot—and what's not—in real-estate investing. What are the hot markets?

Danter: "Every year we put together a list of what's hot and what's not from information we gather for 150 metropolitan areas.

"Some findings that might interest you: Boston dropped from last year's top 15 list. It went from 15th in 1986 to 43rd in 1987.

"New to the top 15 in 1987 was Birmingham, Alabama. New to the bottom 15 was the Charlotte, North Carolina area.

"Houston, which has occupied a spot near the bottom for several years, has been steadily moving up due to sharply reduced construction for the past two years.

"Most improved markets were Oklahoma City (Oklahoma), Denver (Colorado), Baton Rouge (Louisiana), Kansas City (Missouri), and Corpus Christi (Texas). Many of these markets' improvements were due to lack of new starts following a period of overbuilding, rather than increased demand.

"We noted major declines in development opportunity—created by two to three years of accelerated development in the Minneapolis/St. Paul (Minnesota) area, San Diego and Sacramento (California), and Indianapolis (Indiana).

"On our 'what's hot' list—in alphabetical order—are Anaheim/Santa Ana (California), Birmingham (Alabama), Buffalo (New York), Cleveland (Ohio), Columbus (Ohio), Detroit (Michigan), El Paso (Texas), and Los Angeles/Long Beach (California).

"Also on our list: Louisville (Kentucky), Miami/Hialeah (Florida), Milwaukee (Wisconsin), Nassau/Suffolk (New York), Salt Lake City/Ogden (Utah), San Antonio (Texas), San Francisco (California), and San Jose (California)."

What's not hot?

Danter: "On our 'what's not hot' list—in alphabetical order—are Atlanta and Augusta (Georgia), Austin (Texas), Charleston (South Carolina), Charlotte (North Carolina), Colorado Springs (Colorado), Dallas (Texas), and Daytona Beach (Florida).

"Also, Fort Lauderdale/Hollywood (Florida), Fort Worth/Arlington (Texas), Greensboro/Winston-Salem (North Carolina), Houston (Texas), Huntsville (Alabama), Jacksonville (Florida), Johnstown (Pennsylvania), and Lawrence (Massachusetts).

"Melbourne/Titusville/Cocoa (Florida), Memphis (Tennessee), Middlesex/Somerset/Hunterdon (New Jersey), Minneapolis/St. Paul (Minnesota), Monmouth/Ocean (New Jersey), Nashville (Tennessee), Norfolk/Virginia Beach/Newport News (Virginia), and Orlando (Florida).

"In addition, Pensacola (Florida), Phoenix (Arizona), Raleigh/Durham (North Carolina), Richmond/Petersburg (Virginia), Riverside/San Bernardino (California), San Diego (California), Santa Rosa/Petaluma (California), and St. Louis (Missouri).

"Finally, Tampa/St. Petersburg/Clearwater (Florida), Trenton (New Jersey), Tucson (Arizona), Tulsa (Oklahoma), Vallejo/Fairfield/Napa (California), Washington (District of Columbia), West Palm Beach/Boca Raton (Florida), and Worcester (Massachusetts) are not hot."

We'll talk more about the outlook for specific real-estate markets later. What types of real-estate investments are hot now?

Hill: "Regional shopping centers are still hot. You have to tolerate cash-flow returns in the 5-percent to 6.5-percent range to buy one.

"Right now, I also like solid cash-flow properties, such as apartments and warehouses, many of which are priced to deliver yields in the 8- to 11-percent range."

Danter: "Second homes are hot."

You say the market for second homes is heating up?

Danter: "The growth market that we see right now is in condominium rentals—investor condominiums. And we're seeing that growth in most markets."

Every few years, it seems, there's a trendy real-estate investment.

First, it was time-sharing. Now, it's vacation condominiums.

Danter: "I don't think investor condominiums are as trendy as time-sharing. The people who invest in vacation condos are investing some serious bucks. It's not uncommon for an investor to go into a single complex and buy a dozen units."

Any tips for selecting a vacation condominium that you intend to rent?

Danter: "Look at the strength of management—check whether it's maintaining and marketing the condominiums in a professional manner, meaning it competes on the level of motels and hotels for customers."

We know what's hot and what's not. Now, let's talk about how investors put their money into real estate. What are the options today?

Hindman: "They're the same now as they were before the stock-market crash. Investors have essentially three options for investing in real estate.

"The first option is to purchase securities of real-estate companies—you invest in, say, a real-estate investment trust (REIT).

"The second option is to invest in a limited partnership. The partnership buys and manages the property, and you hold an ownership stake.

"The third and final option is to purchase property directly—that is, you can buy residential rental property or land or commercial real estate yourself."

In the past, people invested in real-estate limited partnerships for the tax losses. That's not the case anymore, is it?

Danter: "That's right. The real-estate industry can't sell investors losses anymore. Since the passage of the 1986 Tax Reform Act, we're in a totally new environment.

"For years, the real-estate industry won by losing.

"We've had people who, for years, had a reputation for being good. But they were good only because they were losing—not because they were winning."

Have investors turned away from investing in passive real-estate deals—that is, limited partnerships—in the wake of tax reform?

Moody: "No. It may surprise you—it did me—but more money flowed into public, real-estate limited partnerships in 1987 than in 1986."

But the deals are different?

Moody: That's right. We've shifted from leveraged to nonleveraged deals. These deals offer current income, and they aren't tax-motivated or tax-structured."

We haven't discussed raw land? How does it look as an investment?

Greenfield: "Raw land is on the speculative end of the real-estate investment spectrum. If the economy is soft, the land is soft."

What precisely is a REIT?

Greenfield: "REITs are securities of companies whose principal business is owning and managing real estate. The securities are publicly traded, primarily on the New York Stock Exchange (NYSE) and the American Stock Exchange (ASE).

"Rockefeller Center, for example, is a REIT traded on the New York Stock Exchange, and most of the suburban shopping malls that ring the major cities are owned by somebody on the NYSE."

How do REITs work?

Greenfield: "Usually there's a board of trustees. The trustees own the properties and collect the rents and pay the taxes.

"The cash flow of the properties over and above expenses—and that includes the mortgages—is paid out to the shareholders of the REITS.

"Dividends are based on cash flows, not earnings."

What's a REIT fund?

Greenfield: "A real-estate fund is simply a collection of securities like any other mutual fund. Our fund—before expenses—has a yield of about 9 percent."

What are the advantages of REITs?

Moody: "When you invest in a REIT, you're buying more than a piece of an existing portfolio. You're investing in a development company that continues to add assets to the portfolio. You also have liquidity. You have liquidity from day one."

Rudoff: "Also with a REIT, you don't have to worry that every time there's a new tax bill, your investment is going to be attacked."

What's the advantage of a REIT fund?

Greenfield: "You have diversification. If a fund holds a portfolio of 70 stocks, and each of those stocks holds, maybe, 50 properties, you're really investing in 500 properties.

"And if there's a vacancy someplace, it may not even hurt that particular stock. But even if it does, you have 49 other stocks that are doing well. So the mutual fund concept of spreading the risk and spreading the portfolio geographically works."

Should people invest in REITs or REIT funds for income or capital appreciation?

Greenfield: "In a period of inflation—like we had back in the early 1980s—REITs are a hedge, just like oil or gold. And they provide appreciation. In a period of falling or stable interest rates, REITs provide investors with income.

"Figure on REITs as long-term investments. You should put your money in and forget about it for five to 15 years, not two or three years."

How did REITs and REIT funds weather the crash?

Greenfield: "In the crash, our fund's net asset value went down less than half as fast as the market. For every $10 the market went down, we went down $4.50.

"Since October, utilities, telephone stocks, and real estate have been among the top performers. For the year, real-estate stocks are in the top 20 percent of all stocks."

Any tips for investors in REITs?

Frank: "Real estate is a regional business. So we look for strong regional operating companies with a focus. We think that the people who are going to do the best investing in the Middle Atlantic states, say, are the people who are there.

"Then, people say, well, 'If you're just in one area, how do you get diversification?' We suggest you get diversification by buying another company in another area. That way, you can really get diversification and also get liquidity in the bargain.

"We also look for self-administration—that is, the management is employed by the trust. That way, the management has a reason to enhance the value of the existing properties.

"We also look for prudent financial management. And we look for trusts that are buying properties at amounts below appraised value."

Track records are important, too, right?

Frank: "That's right. Look at the results. REITs are all public companies, so information is readily available.

"How has the company done? How has it fared after it acquired new properties? Ask those types of questions. They'll help you evaluate the company properly."

What are the advantages of limited partnerships?

Frank: "The law doesn't restrict the partnership's activities—whether that activity is the sale, management, or development of property. With REITs, the law does impose restrictions."

How do you evaluate a partnership?

Rudoff: "You only want to invest with people who have good track records, who've been in the business for a number of years, know the marketplace, and have good property management skills. But remember, you generally have no liquidity with a partnership share. So you better be sure you're doing a darn good job of knowing what you're investing in."

Frank: "Read the offering circular, and read about the partnership's investment objective. Is it current income? Is it long-term capital appreciation?

"Also, check out the sponsor. Does the sponsor have a track record? How many other programs has the sponsor been involved in? How well have the projects done?"

OUTLOOK

What's the outlook for real estate across the country? You'll find the answers—region by region—in the section that follows. One note: Average prices of existing rental houses and data on price appreciation come from Monte Helme of Century 21.

Northeast

Experts: Monte Helme, vice president, Century 21; Kenneth Danter, president, Kenneth Danter & Co.; John S. Moody, president and chief executive officer, PaineWebber Properties

Comment: "We don't have any flat-out winners in the Northeast," says Danter. "But we don't have any flat-out losers, either.

"The whole Northeast continues to absorb new housing well. So, overall, all the markets in the region are good, despite some short-term overbuilding.

"The second-home market along the coast," he concludes, "is really heating up. That's the most interesting market."

Comment: "Many homeowners in the Boston area," says Helme, "are taking advantage of the rapid appreciation of home values there by refinancing properties and using the equity build-up to purchase vacation homes in nearby resort areas of New Hampshire."

Comment: "The Northeast," says Moody, "is one of the glamor areas of the last several years."

Connecticut: Average price of an existing rental home: $68,532. Appreciation from June 1986 to June 1987: 12 percent.

Maine: Average price of an existing rental home: $68,532. Appreciation from June 1986 to June 1987: 14 percent.

Massachusetts: "Boston is a market that is growing like crazy," says Danter. "But, over the short term, it's overstretching its capacity to absorb new housing. So," he concludes, "it's not on our 'what's hot' list."

Average price of existing rental home: $169,368. Appreciation from June 1986 to June 1987: 20 percent.

New Hampshire: "Property values in the lake country around Laconia, New Hampshire," Helme says, "have appreciated an average of 10 percent to 15 percent annually over the past few years. On some lakefront properties, the appreciation rate has been much greater."

Average price of existing rental home: $104,119. Appreciation from June 1986 to June 1987: 14 percent.

Rhode Island: "The big jump in real-estate values in Rhode Island," Helme says, "is a result of the influx of homebuyers commuting to Boston. Providence is the appreciation leader in the country.

"Rhode Island's Department of Environmental Management estimates that much of the vacant land in Rhode Island will be classified as wetlands unsuitable for development, which should keep the upward pressure on land values in the years ahead."

Average price of existing rental home: $111,388. Appreciation from June 1986 to June 1987: 54 percent.

Vermont: Average price of existing rental home: $73,131. Appreciation from June 1986 to June 1987: 13 percent.

Middle Atlantic

Experts: Monte Helme, vice president, Century 21; Kenneth Danter, president, Kenneth Danter & Co.

Comment: "The Middle Atlantic is a real growth area," says Danter. "There's a lot going on in eastern Pennsylvania, southeastern New York, and New Jersey.

"New York City is a strong market, and it will remain strong, simply because of the absolute volume of people there.

"Also, there's just no place to build. Communities from Poughkeepsie to Trenton are feeling the impact of the dispersal of people and jobs out of the New York City area. Even Philadelphia has a fair amount of commuters to New York.

"So prices are accelerating rapidly.

"The growth, as a region, is predominantly due to internal mobility—people moving from one home to another. What ends up being a gain in Trenton ends up being a loss to someplace else in the region. I don't see a lot of net gain. It's just a restirring of the pot.

"Right now, the area is probably being overbuilt commercially. There are a lot of commercial office buildings that are up and that are being projected. But I think the area is going to continue to be hot for a very long time."

New Jersey: Average price of existing rental home: $122,608. Appreciation from June 1986 to June 1987: 26 percent.

New York: "New York City has a shortage of 60,000 to 70,000 rental units that will never be built," says Danter. "There's just no place to put them.

"The other bright spot there is Buffalo. All you've got to do is watch Monday Night Football in the middle of winter, and you can see why no national developers from the Southwest get interested in Buffalo. But it's a good market.

"When the chips are down, who wants to go to Buffalo and try to build something? Nobody, and the result is a housing shortage.

"We also see a real shift in the Hudson River Valley."

Average price of existing rental home: $93,121. Appreciation from June 1986 to June 1987: 19 percent.

Pennsylvania: "Eastern Pennsylvania's Pocono Mountain resort area has experienced an explosion of property values over the past few years," Helme says. "Appreciation of single family homes is currently running about 25 percent per year.

"Nearly 50 percent of the buyers are from New York or New Jersey. About half of them purchase vacation homes, and the other half buy primary homes here and commute.

"The buyers are attracted by lower taxes and the much lower housing prices in the Poconos. The average home price in northern New Jersey's Westchester County is $301,000, while primary residences in the Poconos sell for an average of $130,000. Vacation homes start at around $85,000."

Pennsylvania: Average price of existing rental home: $55,621. Appreciation from June 1986 to June 1987: 9.5 percent.

South Atlantic

Experts: Monte Helme, vice president, Century 21; Kenneth Danter, president, Kenneth Danter & Co.

Comment: "There's only one city in the South Atlantic states—Miami—that's on our 'what's hot' list," says Danter. "And there are a bunch of cities on our 'what's not hot' list. The South Atlantic region," he states flatly, "is overbuilt."

Delaware: Average price of existing rental home: $65,102. Appreciation from June 1986 to June 1987: 7 percent.

Florida: "Eleven cities in Florida are on our 'what's not hot' list," says Danter. "These cities are Boca Raton, Clearwater, Cocoa, Jacksonville, Melbourne, Orlando, Pensacola, Tampa, Titusville, St. Petersburg, and West Palm Beach."

"Condo prices have also dropped dramatically in the Tampa, Florida, area due to overbuilding," says Helme. "Two-bedroom condos start in the mid-$40,000 range, with waterfront properties $100,000 and up. Investors can find good deals right now.

"In Jacksonville," Helme continues, "two- and three-bedroom beachfront condos are available in the $110,000 to $150,000 price range."

Average price of existing rental home: $62,625. Appreciation from June 1986 to June 1987: 6 percent.

Maryland: Average price of existing rental home: $77,499. Appreciation from June 1986 to June 1987: 6 percent.

North Carolina: "The cities in North Carolina that are on our 'not hot' list," Danter says, "are Charlotte, Greensboro, High Point, Raleigh-Durham, and Winston-Salem.

"Take a market like Raleigh. You'd think with the amount of press it gets that there are two million people in Raleigh. But it's a relatively small community with tremendous growth. And it is overbuilt in response to that growth.

"What has happened in Raleigh is that you have a higher vacancy rate. So you have rental giveaways, and you have longer absorption periods for new buildings. The good news about Raleigh," he concludes, "is that absorption hasn't stopped altogether."

Average price of existing rental home: $60,214. Appreciation from June 1986 to June 1987: 4.5 percent.

South Carolina: "Charleston is on our 'what's not hot' list," says Danter. "So are those parts of South Carolina near Augusta, Georgia, and Charlotte, North Carolina."

Average price of existing rental home: $58,219. Appreciation from June 1986 to June 1987: 0.

Virginia: Average price of existing rental home: $69,374. Appreciation from June 1986 to June 1987: 8 percent.

East North Central

Experts: Monte Helme, vice president, Century 21; Kenneth Danter, president, Kenneth Danter & Co.

Comment: "The East North Central region is an area that's been overlooked for a long, long time," says Danter. "We don't have any losers in that area at all.

"Five of the cities on our 'what's hot' list—Chicago, Cleveland, Columbus, Detroit, and Milwaukee—are in the region, which is basically the rust belt.

"Close to half the people in the country live in the region. And virtually all the cities can support more housing than they have had in the past.

"Now, some of those cities—Columbus is one and Detroit is another—are coming very close to peaking out. But they're not there yet. There are still some opportunities. Virtually across the board in those states, there is no really bad city right now.

"Another point: We're seeing a real resurgence in the Great Lakes in the second-home market. The Great Lakes—particularly Lake Michigan and Lake Erie—are back."

Illinois: "The greater Chicago market is always diverse enough that the economic cycles won't affect it as much as they do the rest of the Midwest," says Helme.

"A pent-up demand for real estate is expected to strengthen as both homebuyers and investors benefit from continued low interest rates and increased buying power.

"Price appreciation has remained level in office space, but the strong local economy has kept leasing and absorption rates strong."

Moody agrees. "Chicago," he says, "remains strong."

Average price of existing rental home: $74,351. Appreciation from June 1986 to June 1987: 8.9 percent.

Indiana: Average price of existing rental home: $52,130. Appreciation from June 1986 to June 1987: 9 percent.

Michigan: Average price of existing rental home: $44,921. Appreciation from June 1986 to June 1987: 4 percent.

Ohio: "We have close to 2 million people in Cleveland," says Danter. "They have the same desire for a new home that people in Raleigh and Tampa do. So you have an immense amount of demand throughout that area and a shortage of housing."

Cincinnati and Columbus are Helme's picks as markets of opportunity in Ohio.

"Cincinnati is a strong Midwest city with a well-diversified economy that appears to have a stable, healthy future," says Helme. "Unlike some of its Midwest cousins, Cincinnati is without a strong dependence on automobile-related industries.

"The city has a large inventory of office space, but prices have remained stable. Residential rental vacancies are under 10 percent in most areas, and rents have remained stable. Employment growth has been strong over the past four years and is expected to continue.

"Columbus is a sister city to Cincinnati. It has had a strong period of growth for the past four to five years. Economic diversification is once again the name of the game. Columbus is now the largest city—population wise—in Ohio.

"The city has a pretty well-balanced employment base, and its economy is really not susceptible to those Midwestern economic swings."

Average price of existing rental home: $47,774. Appreciation from June 1986 to June 1987: 2 percent.

Wisconsin: "Many investors from Chicago and Milwaukee have bought vacation homes in the Eagle River, Wisconsin, area," Helme reports, "where prices start around $35,000."

Average price of existing rental home: $45,042. Appreciation from June 1986 to June 1987: 0.

East South Central

Experts: Monte Helme, vice president, Century 21; Kenneth Danter, president, Kenneth Danter & Co.

Comment: "We have a couple of real winners in the East South Central states," says Danter. "Birmingham is one. Louisville is another. And there are two markets with surplus construction—Memphis and Nashville. The rest of the region is tougher to get a handle on.

"Some of the markets are overbuilt. Some are not. It's an area with few flashy cities, so it hasn't attracted developers. Also, it's depressed economically."

Alabama: "Birmingham is on our 'what's hot' list," says Danter. "It is more an industrial community than it is a typical sunbelt community. And I don't think it had the flash and chrome to excite a lot of developers in terms of growth. So there's room for development now."

Average price of existing rental home: $53,006. Appreciation from June 1986 to June 1987: 10 percent.

Georgia: "Atlanta continues to be the focus of activity in the region," Helme reports. "It's a transportation hub, a cultural center, a strong, healthy market, and a booming business and service center.

"Prices on office space have remained stable and strong over the past year. Vacancies have risen recently in multifamily units, but the economy is strong, and investors continue to be attracted to the city.

"Although vacancies in office space have risen recently, local real-estate professionals continue to be positive and optimistic about Atlanta's future."

Average price of existing rental home: $65,388. Appreciation from June 1986 to June 1987: 10 percent.

Kentucky: "Louisville," Danter says, "is one of those cities that, until recently, was overlooked by the developers, so it's a hot market now."

Average price of existing rental home: $45,583. Appreciation from June 1986 to June 1987: 1.5 percent.

Mississippi: Average price of existing rental home: $48,015. Appreciation from June 1986 to June 1987: 0.

Tennessee: "Early on," says Danter, "National developers came out of the Southwest into Memphis and began to build. It's overbuilt, and it hasn't recovered from the development blitz yet. There are some real problems there."

Average price of existing rental home: $54,512. Appreciation from June 1986 to June 1987: 12 percent.

West Virginia: Average price of existing rental home: $45,277. Appreciation from June 1986 to June 1987: 2.6 percent.

West North Central

Experts: Monte Helme, vice president, Century 21; Kenneth Danter, president, Kenneth Danter & Co.

Comment: "Two cities in the West North Central are on our 'what's not hot' list," says Danter, "Minneapolis and St. Louis. They are overbuilt markets.

"The good thing about both of them, however, is that they were underbuilt for so long, the deficits were so strong, that we were able to overbuild in both markets without any devastating impact.

"In many of these cities, what will really tell the story is what happens in the first six months of 1988. We had a real gap in construction starts in the first six months of 1987, because everybody held back in their planning, not knowing the impact of the Tax Reform Act.

"So what happens through the first six months of 1988 is going to be important in terms of which way the markets go. A lot of cities there are on the cusp and could go either way."

Iowa: Average price of existing rental home: $36,997. Appreciation from June 1986 to June 1987: 2 percent.

Kansas: Average price of existing rental home: $50,863. Appreciation from June 1986 to June 1987: 3 percent.

Minnesota: Average price of existing rental home: $47,934. Appreciation from June 1986 to June 1987: 5 percent.

Missouri: "Because of its diversified employment base," says Helme, "Kansas City has been able to support a continued absorption of office space that has become available due to a high rate of construction. Kansas City is a market worthy of investigation for investors."

Average price of existing rental home: $45,179. Appreciation from June 1986 to June 1987: 11.6 percent.

Nebraska: Average price of existing rental home: $47,280. Appreciation from June 1986 to June 1987: 0.

North Dakota: Average price of existing rental home: $40,576. Appreciation from June 1986 to June 1987: Declined.

South Dakota: Average price of existing rental home: $45,850. Appreciation from June 1986 to June 1987: 20 percent.

West South Central

Experts: Monte Helme, vice president, Century 21; Kenneth Danter, president, Kenneth Danter & Co., Barry A. Greenfield, vice president, Fidelity Investments, and manager of Fidelity Real Estate Investment Portfolio.

Comment: "Texas, Oklahoma, Louisiana, and Arkansas are in pretty bad shape," says Danter. "Basically, everything there is overbuilt.

"Houston, Austin, Dallas, Tulsa are all in bad shape. They're showing signs of recovery. But they still have a long way to go.

"Some of the other markets in the region, because they were smaller to start with and were jumped over by the developers, may recover a little quicker.

"I think, though, that the problems in Houston, Dallas, and Tulsa are going to overshadow everything in that region for a while.

"If you're in this area, be very, very careful."

Arkansas: Average price of existing rental home: $45,845. Appreciation from June 1986 to June 1987: 7.5 percent.

Louisiana: Average price of existing rental home: $51,761. Appreciation from June 1986 to June 1987: 1.5 percent.

Oklahoma: "In Durant, Oklahoma, near the famous bass fishing area of Texahoma Lake, prices have dropped about 20 percent across the board due to the oil glut," says Helme.

Average price of existing rental home: $47,916. Appreciation from June 1986 to June 1987: 0.

Texas: "Houston has gone from 60,000 to 70,000 new housing starts a year to 5,000 to 6,000 starts," Danter says. "There's a lot of housing product in Houston that was poorly conceived and should never have been built.

"If you take that product out, the market may not be as bad as we think for good product. But we're still some time away from making anything happen there.

"We've advised some clients to go to Houston and buy property. You can buy it for 50 cents on the dollar. And if you buy right, there are some good opportunities.

"The problem with this market, however, is that at the first sign of something positive going on, there's a dozen people who can jump in and overbuild it in a month.

"So you have to be very careful with this strategy. It's a game for real professionals. Remember, even at 50 cents on the dollar, some property is overpriced."

Says Moody: "I'm from Houston, and I know that market well. There are definite values there. But you are not going to go there and make a killing in a year or two.

"But if you have a seven- to ten-year view of real estate, which is the only view to have—you'll wake up and find that you've made money.

"Houston," he concludes, "is not going to blow away."

Says Greenfield: "Houston is probably the cheapest place to invest now. Houston doesn't need any more office buildings, but, believe it or not, they're chewing through their housing inventory. And housing prices are going up in Houston."

Average price of existing rental home: $58,781. Appreciation from June 1986 to June 1987: Declined.

Mountain

Experts: Monte Helme, vice president, Century 21; Kenneth Danter, president, Kenneth Danter & Co.

Comment: "In this region," Danter says, "cities are few and far between. Nevertheless, the national developers have hit the region.

"Phoenix and Tuscon are now overbuilt. Colorado Springs is overbuilt. Denver has been overbuilt for a long time but is showing some signs of recovery. We're still a year or two away from having a decent market there. Salt Lake City is the best market out there."

Arizona: Average price of existing rental home: $67,637. Appreciation from June 1986 to June 1987: 0.

Colorado: "Colorado's Rocky Mountain ski areas have experienced dramatic declines in property values since the peaks reached in the early 1980s," says Helme. "So investors now have an opportunity to buy vacation homes at lower prices.

"In Frisco, near Breckenridge and other prime ski areas, prices have dropped about 40 percent over the past five years. Condo prices range from a low of around $30,000 up to $1 million, depending largely on their location and newness. The average is about $100,000."

Says Moody: "I think there are some very good buys for patient money, for the long-view investor in Denver."

Average price of existing rental home: $65,148. Appreciation from June 1986 to June 1987: 6 percent.

Idaho: Average price of existing rental home: $45,038. Appreciation from June 1986 to June 1987: 6 percent.

Montana: Average price of existing rental home: $45,939. Appreciation from June 1986 to June 1987: 5 percent.

New Mexico: Average price of existing rental home: $60,968. Appreciation from June 1986 to June 1987: 6 percent.

Utah: Average price of existing rental home: $59,264. Appreciation from June 1986 to June 1987: 5 percent.

Wyoming: "The oil glut has also affected values in the Jackson area," says Helme, "where home and condo prices have dropped about 30 percent since 1980, 1981. Prices have stabilized now. Condo prices start at $45,000 and single-family homes at $60,000 to $65,000."

Average price of existing rental home: $53,312. Appreciation from June 1986 to June 1987: 11 percent.

West

Experts: Monte Helme, vice president, Century 21; Kenneth Danter, president, Kenneth Danter & Co.

Comment: "The West Coast is a mixed bag," says Danter. "We don't have any really bad markets there. But we don't have any really good markets, either. Portland and Seattle have to be the lead cities, just in terms of their capacity to absorb new housing."

"The West," says Moody, "is another one of the glamor areas of the last few years."

Alaska: Average price of existing rental home: $91,250. Appreciation from June 1986 to June 1987: Declined.

California: "Some markets—San Diego, Santa Rosa—got overbuilt in a hurry," says Danter. "On the other hand, some of the big markets—Los Angeles, San Francisco—are still very good. Because of the sheer volume of the population, we've not been able to keep up with demand."

Average price of existing rental home: $106,305. Appreciation from June 1986 to June 1987: 7 percent.

Hawaii: "On Hawaii's Kona-Kohala 'gold coast,' average condo prices have dropped from $250,000 a few years ago to about $150,000 today," Helme notes.

"Meanwhile, rental rates have increased from an average of $400 a month to about $1,200 a month for a two- or three-bedroom unit.

"Single-family home prices start at $90,000. Our midrange single-family market, priced from $150,000 to $250,000, is beginning to move again."

Average price of existing rental home: $154,263. Appreciation from June 1986 to June 1987: 39 percent.

Nevada: "In the Lake Tahoe area, prices have stabilized after a period of decline," says Helme. "Single-family homes start at around $100,000 and condos at $60,000."

Average price of existing rental home: $81,327. Appreciation from June 1986 to June 1987: 2.5 percent.

Oregon: "Portland is one of the better markets for elderly housing that we've had occasion to look at in some time," says Danter.

Average price of existing rental home: $44,883. Appreciation from June 1986 to June 1987: 2 percent.

Washington: Average price of existing rental home: $58,468. Appreciation from June 1986 to June 1987: 8 percent.

7

HIDDEN TREASURE
The Outlook for Hard Assets

The tangible reality of hard assets—oil in the ground, for instance, or gold in a vault—doesn't assure one who invests in them of absolute safety and stability.

But when times become more uncertain than they ordinarily are, these hard assets can begin to look awfully good. Are they? Should your portfolio include investments in natural resources? And what about gold, that favorite long-term haven?

In this chapter, we'll find out what the experts say about the current advisability of hard assets. They'll tell us where they think the price of gold is heading and what the outlook is for oil and natural gas.

They'll also tell us about alternative ways of making these investments. Do you buy stock in a gold mining company or purchase the metal itself? In discussing oil and gas investments, what's the difference between exploratory programs, development programs, balanced programs, and income programs?

There's a reason why hard assets start to look attractive when the unpredictable winds of financial change start to blow. Read on to learn why.

Our experts in the hard-asset category include:

- Jean-Marie Eveillard, portfolio manager of the Sogen International Fund, a top-performing mutual fund based in New York City.
- Robert A. Hewitt, Jr., a financial planner in the offices of Christopher Weil & Co., a financial planning firm based in Monterey, California.
- James A. C. Kennedy III, vice president and director of research for T. Rowe Price Associates, an investment management company in Baltimore, Maryland.
- John D. Markese, vice president and research director for the American Association of Individual Investors based in Chicago.
- J. Clarence Morrison, first vice president and senior metals analyst for Dean Witter Reynolds, a brokerage firm in New York City.
- Arnold G. Rudoff, president, Rudoff & Co., investment advisers specializing in partnerships. The company is based in Menlo Park, California.
- Sean St. Clair, metals industry analyst for Chicago-based Duff & Phelps, investment advisers.
- Anthony M. Sorrentino, metals industry analyst for Standard & Poor's, an investment advisory company headquartered in New York City.
- Arch Spencer, manager of the IDS Precious Metals Fund and the IDS New Dimensions Fund for IDS Financial Services in Minneapolis.

Here's what our experts had to say.

Let's start with gold. What were you telling investors about gold and gold stocks before the crash?

Morrison: "We had gold in the hold/sell category. We felt that bullion prices were heading lower because of heavy central bank selling. We also thought gold equities were out of line with bullion prices—dramatically out of line."

How did gold-oriented stocks fare in the crash?

St. Clair: "Gold really hasn't changed much at all. But gold equities are down 35 percent to 40 percent. It seems to be an excessive overreaction."

Did investors flee to gold after the crash?

Spencer: "No."

Has the price of gold increased since the crash?

Spencer: "No. It just sat there."

Why hasn't the price increased?

Spencer: "Gold will go up only if we have a real financial panic. I don't call the crash a financial panic.

"We haven't had any banks close. We haven't had any big brokerage firms go bankrupt. We haven't had any stock exchanges ceasing activity, except maybe Hong Kong's.

"In short, we haven't had the kind of panic that would scare people toward gold. What we had was a stock market decline of about 20 percent."

Eveillard: "We had two offsetting forces. One was the fear of recession, which was bearish for gold. Second was the tremendous uncertainty, related to the crash, that was bullish for gold. So these two factors offset one another. Gold, the metal, behaved in a very boring way, barely moving.

"Gold did not play its traditional role of refuge, because, all of a sudden, we were introducing—wrongly in my opinion, but only time will tell—the idea of imminent recession."

So is gold overpriced?

Spencer: "The price of gold is in line with the dollar. In the United States, it has appreciated because our dollar has depreciated."

St. Clair: "You can make a basic Economics 101 comparison and come to the conclusion that gold is overpriced, given new supplies coming on line in the United States, Canada, and Australia.

"But the economic argument doesn't seem to have a whole lot of influence on the underlying gold prices. People view gold as a safe haven. And it has other intrinsic qualities that make it act differently from other industrial metals."

Where do you see the price of gold heading?

Sorrentino: "It depends on the economy. If the economy slows down or we enter a recession, gold prices will probably stay flat or head lower."

Eveillard: "Over the next six to twelve months, I think the price of gold will go up. If I'm right and there's no recession and inflation accelerates, I certainly believe that it can get between $500 and $600 an ounce, maybe higher."

Morrison: "We said in print that we expected gold would average around $430 in 1987, and it's going to average around $440. We've been saying, and we've been saying for some time, that gold may average lower in 1988 than in 1987. We haven't changed our opinion.

"But we expect 1989 gold pricing to be dramatically higher—averaging somewhere between $500 and $550 an ounce."

So should people invest in gold now?

Markese: "For most people, the volatility of these investments, given their yield, doesn't make them worthwhile. The only time they perform well is in runaway inflation."

Spencer: "I'd use gold as a hedge only. Five to 15 percent of your assets should be in gold, at most."

Hewitt: "If gold or precious metals have a place in a person's portfolio, I'd say no more than 5 to 10 percent. If we have a client who wants to invest in gold, my first inclination is to tell him or her to buy gold jewelry, put some diamonds in it, and enjoy it."

Sorrentino: "It's not time yet."

Does gold really work as a hedge?

Spencer: "Well, the market is flat for the year. At IDS, our bond fund is down for the year. And our gold fund is up about 35 percent. So it is a hedge. It's protection against something that didn't happen this time—a real financial crisis."

What type of investor should put money in gold?

Sorrentino: "A fairly aggressive investor, someone younger rather than older, someone who is fairly well off with extra money to speculate."

If now is not the time to buy gold, when is the time to buy?

Sorrentino: "There could be two scenarios that would be favorable for gold prices. In the first, the economy picks up again after a slowdown.

"If growth in the economy accelerated, I would expect the rate of inflation to pick up, and higher inflation would lead to increased gold prices.

"The other scenario? We go into a recession, which deepens to the point where there are concerns about the stability of the financial system. At that point, gold would be a good investment."

When you say gold, do you mean both gold and gold stocks?

Sorrentino: "Gold stocks are a little more questionable. On the one hand, they would build up with the gold price. On the other hand, in the last scenario I described, they probably would be strained to some extent by a weakening stock market.

"I think we can assume that if there are concerns about the financial system, the stock market would be declining at that point."

Say I'm an investor, and I've decided that gold is the ticket. Should I invest in gold or gold stocks?

Spencer: "Instead of buying gold, I'd buy the companies that produce the gold. Many stocks in Australia are selling for a third of what they were selling for in September."

Kennedy: "With stocks, you profit from the unit growth as well as the leverage from the price of gold. Take Newmont Gold. It was producing 300,000 ounces a year, and now its potential is about 1.6 million ounces a year by 1990. That's tremendous unit growth."

Eveillard: "The only way to own gold in a conservative manner is to own the metal itself. Stocks are not a conservative way to own gold."

Mr. Spencer, which does your fund invest in—gold or gold stocks?

Spencer: "Stocks. We had the metals before, but I sold them and put the money in the gold stocks."

Why?

Spencer: "Stock prices appreciate about twice as fast as gold prices. So you stand to gain more. Of course, you also stand to lose more."

Do the prices of gold stocks move in tandem with the price of gold?

St. Clair: "They usually do. But during this cycle, gold leveled out, while gold equities continued to climb. The spread between where the equities and gold usually trade became abnormal, and the gold equities became too pricey. That imbalance was corrected in the crash."

Morrison: "I think gold bullion prices and gold equities will have a much closer price correlation than they had in 1987. That's been one of the problems. The stocks got dramatically out of line with gold itself."

What's your outlook for gold stocks now?

Morrison: "We have them in a buy/hold category."

Any tips for investors in gold stocks?

Morrison: "There are three keys. One, what are the company's production costs per ounce of gold? Two, what are the company's costs of finding gold per ounce? And three, what are the company's interest charges per ounce?

"In other words, has the company enhanced the shareholder's position by exploring and adding to its reserve position?"

Let's talk about oil and natural gas. The least risky way to invest in oil and gas is to purchase shares of stock in a large oil company, right?

Rudoff: "That's right."

The outlook for oil depends, in large measure, on the price of crude oil. Where do you see the price of crude heading?

Rudoff: "I read in the paper the other day that oil is going back down to $15 a barrel. Then, further on in the column, it said that after oil goes down to $15 a barrel, it is shooting right back up again, because OPEC is going to get control of the situation.

"In short, nobody really knows where oil is heading. So it's hard to justify putting much money directly into oil and gas deals for the average individual."

Mr. Rudoff, you sound totally bearish.

Rudoff: "I'm not totally bearish. I'm not bearish for people who are in the oil business or for those investors who are well-diversified. Oil and gas can have a small place in the portfolios of investors who already own stocks, bonds, real estate, and so on. I know that there are some major institutions, both corporations and pension and endowment funds, that are buying very heavily in the oil business.

"But I'm always bearish for the individual investor, the little guy, who has to pay a big load. If, however, you're going in on close to a straight-up basis, meaning you're not paying a big load, oil and gas can be a good investment."

Is now the time to invest in oil and gas?

Hewitt: "I have been looking at oil and gas for the last two years. And I'm closer to recommending it today than I was two years ago.

"I'd say we're at or near the bottom. I would recommend oil and gas if I could see some hard evidence that we're going to stabilize at $20 or higher a barrel—$18 to $20 is still a little iffy with me.

"So I'd rather wait and see."

There are lots of ways to invest in oil and gas. So let's run through the different types of investments, starting with exploratory programs.

Rudoff: "With exploratory programs, you're drilling for oil as opposed to buying existing production. You're drilling in areas not surrounded by proven wells and looking for new fields.

"Exploratory wells carry the highest risk, and, to me, they're only for people in the oil business. Rarely do individual investors ever get in on exploratory wells that make any economic sense, because the risk is so great—maybe one in ten or one in twenty hit.

"Exploratory programs are strictly for people who are doing a large number of wells each year and can spread the risk over many, many wells. The average investor can't.

"The drilling fund actually got started with a heavy emphasis on exploratory wells, but most investors lost all their money.

"In any case, there's very little being done now in exploratory areas for the average investor. Most of the exploration is really being done by the big oil companies."

What about development programs?

Rudoff: "With development programs, you're drilling within a proven field, so there's a reasonable prospect of finding oil or gas. You'll have success—that is, you'll find oil and gas—50 to 90 percent of the time.

"But finding oil and gas is not the issue in a development program. The issue is getting an economical well. That means getting a payout of money, a return on your investment, within a reasonable period of time.

"The rough guideline is that you should get your money back within five years. But people in the oil business say you should get your money back within two to two-and-a-half years. And they will drill development wells only where they have that kind of a prospect.

"Another important point: Promoters want to show a very good track record, and they usually gauge their track records in terms of successful wells.

"So they tend to drill in areas that professional oil people don't necessarily favor. For example, they may drill in Ohio and Pennsylvania. In many parts of those states, you get good production the first year or so, then it drops off precipitously. The promoter can report a strike, but it's not a very economical well. It could take you ten to twenty years to get your money back."

What about balanced programs?

Rudoff: "A balanced program is just a mix of exploratory and development wells. Again, most of the drilling programs have not worked out very well for investors. So I would caution people against entering into these deals."

Last on the list is income programs.

Rudoff: "With income programs, you're buying a working interest in wells that have already been drilled. So you don't have any of the exploratory risk. Here, the question is, how good a job are the engineers doing when you buy?

"Are you getting in at a favorable price? What's going to happen to the value of the oil in the future? Is the well going to produce for a number of years?

"It's more of an economic analysis than anything else.

"But you still need oil people to evaluate how old the well is, how much oil is left in the ground, and how likely it is that you're going to get what's in the ground out of the ground. And you have to know how much it will cost to get it out. And over how long a period of time."

How do you evaluate these programs?

Rudoff: "When I have an interested client, I hire a petroleum engineer who has at least 10 years experience in the business, and I have the engineer evaluate the deal. The engineer comes up with some reasonable projections, then discounts them heavily for the risks.

"I don't project any increases in the price of oil. If it's $18 a barrel today, we keep it at that price for the life of the investment.

"Once we get the projections, we calculate an internal rate of return number, just as we do with other investments.

"If you're a little investor, that is, you're putting in less than $25,000, say, you're pretty much dependent upon the analysis of the people who are selling you the deal.

"But most people don't know the oil business very well. Some people analyze these deals very well, others don't. So you have to be very, very careful."

What about fees?

Rudoff: "They're all over the board. In most cases, at least 10 percent of the fund is going to the people who raise the money. And there's usually another three or four points going to the people who put the deal together—lawyers, accountants, and so on.

"Then you want to know what kind of a split there will be with the sponsor of the program. With the ideal split, investors get their money back first, then the sponsor takes a piece of it back at, say, 25 percent of the profits.

"But the programs that I see are very mixed. In most cases, the sponsor takes a front-end fee and shares in the income right from the start.

"Most of these sharing arrangements are not very favorable to investors. In fact, the investors get screwed.

"You really have to be well advised in these deals."

What advice would you give potential investors in oil and gas?

Rudoff: "If you really want to be in the oil and gas business—that is, you want to drill wells—invest in the stock of a good oil company or pick a program manager who is well-regarded in the industry and has a good track record going back over five years."

Part III
YOUR PORTFOLIO

8

DO IT NOW
Putting It All Together

Okay. You know how the experts view the stock market's prospects for the next 12 months. And you've read about their outlook for cash, bonds, real estate, and hard assets.

But now you want to know how to put this information all together. What tips do the experts have for constructing a portfolio that will weather future economic storms?

In this chapter, we've asked three leading professionals to outline the basics of sound investing and financial planning. They describe timeless investment strategies—strategies that work in bull and bear markets alike. And they explain how to change your strategies as the economic climate shifts, as it always does.

Our experts for this chapter are:

- Stanley H. Breitbard, national director of executive financial services for Price Waterhouse, a Big Eight accounting firm in New York City.
- Nita Kincaid, senior vice president of retail services for Fidelity Investments, which has its headquarters in Boston.

- John D. Markese, vice president and research director for the American Association of Individual Investors (AAII) in Chicago.

Stanley H. Breitbard

"Financial planning is a way to organize your financial life. You want to develop a plan, then you want to stick to it. And our fundamental thinking on what factors influence your plan hasn't changed as a result of the unsettled market.

"First, you must develop what we call your financial profile—a composite of your stage of life, lifestyle, tolerance for risk, responsibilities, and financial resources. When you develop this profile, you must decide on your main objectives. What are you going to do with your money once you've invested it and made a certain amount of profit?

"Developing objectives means more than saying, 'I'm saving for retirement,' or 'I'm saving for a college education for my children.' You have to put dollar amounts on your objectives and put them in order of importance, because, unfortunately, you're probably going to have many more goals than you can realistically reach.

"Once you've done that initial planning, once you know what's most important to you, you can plot the return you need in order to achieve your major objectives.

"Then you can devise an asset allocation plan. What is asset allocation? It simply means dividing your investable dollars among the different types of investments—cash and cash equivalents, fixed-income instruments, equities, and hard assets.

"You need to develop an asset allocation strategy that makes sense for your stage of life, one that protects you financially by balancing your investments among various instruments so that an ailing market doesn't lead to your financial ruin.

"The whole concept of asset allocation involves strict discipline in the way you invest your dollars, so you don't react emotionally or precipitously when there's either a severe drop like the one we just had, or a sharp rise.

"You also have to put your plans in the perspective of a time horizon and balance them against other parts of your profile—for example, what do you already have in terms of cash flow? What do you have in terms of other kinds of gains, from sales of stock, say?

"Tax aspects also play a part in a person's overall investment strategy. You have to figure out where you can create the most after-tax dollars. And your need for liquidity plays an important role as well in determining the type of investments that make sense for you.

"If you know you're going to need liquidity at specific times, you must allocate parts of your portfolio to enough risk-free or reduced-risk assets, such as cash and cash equivalents. That way you'll have the money you need when you need it.

"You can't be entirely in the equity markets where you may be forced to sell at a time when your assets have dropped 30 percent.

"And, of course, you have to evaluate your tolerance for risk. To help people assess their risk, financial planners use several methods.

"One is to take people through a series of questions about their expectations, asking them what they would be willing to lose versus what they expect to earn from an investment. That kind of question is pretty standard and attempts to quantify where a person stands on a risk-aversion scale.

"We're also experimenting with a method that asks more offbeat questions. For example, what kinds of risks do you take when you're walking down the street?

"Would you usually cross on a red light? Or do you wait for the signal to change? When you're driving on the freeway, how often do you change lanes?

"People can—and should—ask themselves some of these same questions. Are you more interested in income or growth when it comes to your investments? How would you feel if you opened up the financial page and saw that a stock in which you owned a big stake had dropped 20 percent? Would you wish you'd never made the investment?

"The issue today for people looking at the stock market is simply this. Are you comfortable investing in stocks knowing that we could have another crash or simply realizing that the market is very volatile?

"Does the state of the stock market today make you lie awake at night? If it causes you that much discomfort, you should have little or nothing invested in the market.

"So you have to measure risk versus reward. But you also have to take into account dollar levels of risk tolerance.

"Say, for example, that I offer you an incredible bet. I tell you that I'm going to flip a coin. Heads comes up, you pay me $1,000. Tails comes up, I pay you $10,000.

"Would you take the bet? For many people, the answer would be yes, because you have a 50-percent chance of gaining $10,000 and a 50-percent chance of losing $1,000.

"But, say I offered you the same flip of the coin. This time, though, it's heads comes up, you pay me $100,000. Tails, I'll pay you $1 million.

"You'd certainly be tempted. But if you don't have $100,000 to risk, you can't take the bet, no matter how good the odds.

"That's how you have to think about the stock market. You know you have the possibility of getting returns of 12 percent or 15 percent or 20 percent or more. But you also have the risk of a similar decline. So if you can't afford it, proceed with caution.

"Of course, you can mitigate your risk considerably by saying, 'I'm going to put money into this volatile investment over a longer period of time.'

"With a longer-term outlook, you can earn the same return over time as you would in a safer, less risky investment.

"Take somebody who invests in an instrument that returns 8 percent a year for five years in a row. Somebody else invests in a more volatile vehicle. Some years the investment is up 10 percent, some years it's down 25 percent, and some years it's up 40 or 50 percent. But over the five years it returns an average of 8 percent.

"You can construct an infinite number of scenarios. And with any one of them, you may end up with an average annual return of 8 percent. But most people are more comfortable with the investment that *consistently* yields 8 percent.

"Here's the problem with the more volatile portfolio. Say it's up 10 percent in the first year and down 25 percent in the second. Now you get panicky. If you hung in there and stuck with that investment for the next three years, maybe it would go up 50 percent in the next year.

"But in order to achieve that hypothetical 8 percent, you've got to look at your investment as long-term. You have to discipline yourself to stay with it over a period of time. And many people can't. Some can't psychologically, and some can't for practical reasons. They need the money now.

"That's why we definitely have a bias against unnecessary speculation. Speculation brings with it a higher degree of risk. You should strive to achieve your goals and objectives with the minimum amount of risk.

"By taking on more risk than necessary, you subject yourself to wild swings, which can cause you to panic and get out at just the wrong time. The irony is you probably could have achieved the same results had you not speculated, had you not tried to go for an even higher return, perhaps a return that you didn't even need. So think realistically about what return you need to accomplish your objectives, not what sort of return you'd like for cocktail party conversation.

"We can point to lots of statistics to show that diversified portfolios did not come out that badly in the month of October.

"For one reason, when stocks fell, a lot of bonds rose in price. Some of the tangible assets, including real estate, also rose in price.

"Say you had only 30 percent of your assets in common stocks. Even though your stocks may have fallen 25 percent in line with the market average, the effect on your overall portfolio was obviously far less than if you'd been 100 percent invested in equities. People should also keep in mind that diversification doesn't necessarily mean that they're going to have to accept a low return.

"And, hard as it is to believe, 85 percent of your return depends on how you allocate your resources. Only 15 percent depends on your specific investments.

"In fact, over the past 15 years, a diversified portfolio in stocks, bonds, government securities, and real estate has actually outperformed the S&P 500 stock index. How this kind of portfolio performs, of course, depends on the time period you're looking at.

"But at least over this last 15-year time period, you wouldn't have fared badly. Your investment was much more conservative, but your return was actually greater than if you'd been entirely in stocks.

"So mathematically, by diversifying, you can significantly reduce risk without reducing your expected return. And you're reducing volatility as well.

"Of course, with a stock portfolio, you have a chance of getting, perhaps, a 50-percent return in a year. In a diversified portfolio, you have no chance of earning that high a return. But your average return can be fairly close to the average return of the stock market.

"If you have $50,000 or less, by the way, it's difficult to diversify without using mutual funds or some other vehicle that is, in itself, diversified.

"How would you set up a diversified portfolio today?

"First, you must make sure you've provided a liquid fund for emergencies. You should have in that fund from three to six months of your take-home pay.

"Now's a good time, as well, to reassess your financial profile. We've just experienced a tremendous amount of volatility on the downside. Until now, many investors have not experienced what it's like to have risk—not just return—come into play.

"So I think the crash is a good opportunity to sit back and say, 'Am I comfortable assuming the kind of risk that I have been assuming?' It's a good time to zero in on who you are and whether your current financial plan reflects who you are. If you've quantified your objectives and put together a diversified portfolio based on those objectives, I don't recommend going back and reallocating assets just because of the crash.

"If you put the money in the equity market, looking at a long time horizon for those assets to work out, you shouldn't necessarily let the crash scare you away.

"Your objectives haven't changed. Of course, your profile might have shifted. That's a different story. You might think you're a risk taker, but when confronted with something like the crash, you find out you aren't comfortable with risk at all. And if that's the case, you may want to go ahead and change the allocation of your assets.

"But realize that you're not looking at the market's performance so much as you are looking inward. You're realizing you now have an opportunity to reassess your own feelings about risk and reward and volatility."

Nita Kincaid

"When you ask, 'What should investors do now,' the 'now' disturbs me a little. I think that people should really have more long-term plans. They should clearly define the money they need for the 'now' and the money they need for goals down the road.

"People who think about their investment portfolio in that way probably have weathered the storm of the last few months much better than people who react very strongly on a 'now' basis.

"Again, the people who were probably hit the hardest by the downturn in the market are people who forgot an almost basic premise of investing. That is, the dollars you need now, for, say, the down payment on a house, you don't necessarily put in a high-risk investment.

"If somebody said to me, 'I'm going to need this money in two months; what are some of the investments I might put it into?' I would start and probably end with money-market funds. If your investment horizon is that short, you shouldn't take risks unless you have another pot from which you can draw.

"If I needed my money two years down the road, I would certainly put a significant portion in a money-market fund. The most aggressive I would get for a goal with a two-year time horizon would be a growth-and-income fund. And I would probably have a fairly conservative bond fund in the mix as well. That would be my personal approach.

"And money funds, by the way, continue to deliver decent returns for a riskless investment. They got a bad name in that people got so used to 18- and 20-percent rates of return. But the real rate of return on money-market funds versus inflation has, over the past few years, been better generally than it was when money-market funds were paying 18 percent.

"When the markets became increasingly volatile, some people didn't have everything thought through in terms of current dollars that they need and other dollars they're setting aside for future uses.

"One of the things that Fidelity has been doing in customer communications since last spring is stressing the need to have a balanced portfolio. And that suggestion hasn't changed dramatically.

"But the importance of doing so is now clearer to people than it might have been, because we have a lot of investors who really never thought the market could go down.

"It's important that people focus on their goals. And they shouldn't try to always get the last possible dollar from every investment. Certain types of investments are appropriate for certain kinds of objectives, and the individual is the best person to make the decision about whether an investment fits his or her objective right now.

"People reacted differently during the crash. Some were very concerned and made a decision—perhaps because of the amount of dollars they had invested—either very little or a lot—to go very quickly to cash when the market turned down.

"And many people also said, 'Well, this is money that I didn't plan to take out in the near-term anyway. And it would be foolish of me to sell right now. I'm going to ride this out.'

"And then there's another group of people who now suddenly are much more interested in diversifying than they were previously.

"We do a model portfolio series where we say, for example, if you are an aggressive investor, put a small percentage of your assets in a money-market fund, a fairly high percentage in a growth fund, and another percentage in one of the more aggressive growth-and-income funds. And then we have other portfolios for other types of investors.

"But once you decide what kind of an investor you are, you don't shift those percentages. You leave them the same, because those are portfolios for the long term. And eventually, the more aggressive portfolio will deliver higher returns. It will see bigger dips along the way, of course.

"For the next 12 months, I do feel most comfortable across the board with the growth-and-income kind of investments—middle-of-the-road investments. Even during the October period they showed considerably less volatility.

"In any case, I would definitely opt for not putting all my eggs in one basket. It's very trite, but I do think that putting all your money in one kind of investment is a mistake. And I include putting all your money into a CD.

"I wouldn't feel as strongly if it were a short-term CD, but there were plenty of people who got killed when rates went up because they tied their money up in three-year investments.

"If the market smoothes out, I would probably become a little more aggressive.

"People do need to adjust their growth goals, because we really went from 18-percent money-market days into 15- to 20-percent stock days. And bond funds were yielding 8 to 12 percent, plus appreciating in price. So you had phenomenal returns.

"But now people need to adjust their sights downward in terms of the annual growth rate they expect, particularly if they're conservative and the market stays volatile. They need to choose some investments that will be lower risk and, obviously, lower return as well. I'd look for about an 8- to 10-percent return for an entire portfolio.

"As far as safety goes, I do think mutual funds are safer than buying individual stocks. For example, when you compare how a mutual fund did during the crash to the market average, you're coming closer to comparing two similar things.

"Not a lot of investors go out and buy the market average. They buy one or two securities. And the individual investor who goes out and buys just one or two stocks, may or may not have picked stocks that performed as well as the market averages. It depends on how sophisticated they are.

"But if you're not a sophisticated investor, you're better off in a diversified pool of securities. And most people can't afford to do that on their own, or don't have the time.

"But when people go into mutual funds, they should read carefully the description of a fund's objective. And if a fund's objective is growth, they should realize it's going to be much higher risk than if its objective is growth plus income, or if its objective is just current income.

"People are really focused more on past performance numbers. That's not totally wrong. When you're trying to make a decision, you have to look at something that indicates what a fund's performance might be.

"Then you have to add in the ingredient of reality, that says in order for this fund to have gone up 30 percent in the last year when the market went up 25 percent, it obviously took greater risks. And when the market goes down, it could go down more than the market does.

"And I'd certainly look at a fund's performance over more than just one period of time—in up markets and in down.

"The popularity of all the various financial publications and the response we've gotten to our quarterly magazine tells me that there's been a tremendous pick up over the last couple of years in people's interest in their money. And this increased interest probably correlates with the fact that investors saw themselves making more and more money.

"Many times people read financial publications to find an easy answer. But for the next few years, even if the volatility slows down, there aren't going to be as many easy answers.

"People are going to have to work a little harder at their investments. And they won't be able to make big returns without putting a lot of investigation into their investment decisions."

John D. Markese

"If I were designing a portfolio today, here's what I'd do.

"Right now, a reasonable allocation of assets might consist of 50 percent in equities. For many people, high-dividend paying common stocks or equity-income mutual funds make the most sense. I mean funds such as Fidelity's Equity-Income and Puritan funds or the balanced no-load Loomis-Sayles mutual fund.

"These funds, and others like them, go after high-yielding common stocks. Of course, these stocks will fall in a down market. But they fell nowhere near as low as the market in general.

"With equity-income funds, you're still in equities in case the market moves up, but you have the dividend yield to cushion any losses.

"Although it isn't an equity-income fund, I also like the Strong Income Fund. Right now, they're almost all in bonds and cash. The Strong Income Fund—although not an equity-income fund—has performed well.

"And Mutual Shares and Mutual Qualified Shares have been very consistent performers. Both of these funds look for undervalued stock. Also, they do generate some income, so they're not as risky on the downside as many other funds.

"If you're going to choose individual equities, you have to be awfully diversified. You should choose, for the most part, very high-quality, high-dividend paying stocks. And, incidentally, I don't mean just utility industry securities.

"As you can tell, I think people should still be in equities in this market. They just need to take a more conservative approach.

"By the way, I'm not saying people should not be in aggressive growth funds or growth stocks at all. In fact, I think that every portfolio, ideally, should have an aggressive component. But you have to be able to tolerate the risk.

"So if you can tolerate another decline to 1500 or whatever, and can continue to hold onto your investment, and maintain a long-term perspective, you probably should have a portion of your equity allocation in this area. But I worry about the people who buy these investments, get discouraged, and sell off at the bottom.

"Similarly I would argue that any portfolio should have some international representation. The question is, how do you want to achieve this representation?

"Of course, some of the domestic stocks you hold—or some of

the equities in the funds you own—are going to be multinationals anyway. But you could segregate 10 percent of your stock allocation and put it in a global fund or an international fund that's diversified geographically.

"That is, you don't want a fund that includes just the Pacific Basin, say, but one that encompasses both the Pacific Basin and Western Europe. Although people have to realize that the major returns internationally have been from the slide of the dollar. And it isn't likely that the dollar is going to collapse a whole lot more.

"So you're buying these funds for the purpose of further diversifying your portfolio. Your assuming these other economies aren't perfectly tied to ours. But let me emphasize—the massive rates of return in international funds were due to the dollar's fall. And it's hard to believe that's going to continue without all of us going down the tubes.

"As for the other 50 percent of my investable assets, I'd recommend about 25 percent in short-to-intermediate term bond funds and 25 percent in money-market funds. Very simple.

"I do think that money-market funds are the best place to keep cash. They're very flexible. If you see some buying opportunities in individual stocks, or just need the money, you have it. It's easy to get out.

"I'd stay away from CDs—even very short-term ones. They're not worth it. They're not as flexible, because you can't access your money right away. If you want to move on a short-term basis, you can't. You're stuck.

"And unless you have very large sums invested, you're not dealing with a great deal of difference, as far as return is concerned. The dollar amounts you gain are small. And the convenience you give up is substantial.

"I also don't recommend gold for most people. Its volatility, given its yield, is just not worth it.

"The portfolio breakdown I suggest includes all financial assets, including retirement assets. The only asset I exclude is a person's personal residence.

"If someone wanted to start a retirement fund or a fund for a child's education, my recommendation would be the same. That is, it would be the same as long as the person had at least a five-year outlook.

"Of course, I wouldn't necessarily tell people in their twenties or thirties with a 20- or 30- or even 10-year perspective to go heavily into equity income. I'd tell them to slowly pick up some very high-quality aggressive funds—to begin accumulating them.

"But I'm looking here at investors in their forties or fifties. And that's a different game.

"Another point: dollar-cost-averaging—investing regular sums at periodic intervals—makes sense. Never get into the market in one lump sum—and never get out at one point, either. The people who got hurt the most in the crash are the ones who did exactly that.

"You should pull out your money at least over two years. For example, you could divide it into eighths and pull it out, one eighth in each quarter.

"Investing is really simple. It requires planning and diversification and there are no great secrets to it. The big thing is taking the time to form a plan that's appropriate and adhering to it. And that takes discipline and some thought—assessing your risk level, your need for liquidity, your tax situation, and so forth.

"Those fundamentals haven't changed. In fact, if anything, the crash has highlighted them."